GRASS ROOTS

GARDENING

ALSO BY
DONNA SCHAPER

Living Well While Doing Good

A Holy Vulnerability: Spiritual Resources for People With Cancer

Prayers for Easter and Lent

Prayers for Advent and Christmas

Sacred Speech: A Humble How To

When A Parent Dies

Art of Spiritual Rock Gardening

Labyrinths from the Outside In (With Carole Anne Camp)

Prayers for Children

Altar Call

Spiritual Orphans & Spiritual Heirs: Raising Interfaith Children

Sabbath Keeping

All Is Calm

Alone, But Not Lonely1998

Sabbath Sense: A Spiritual Antidote for the Overworked

Why Write Letters?

More Than Bread: The Church and Higher Education

Common Sense About Women in the Ministry

Why I Tithe

Calmly Plotting the Resurrection

Hope for Hard Times: Sermons

Stripping Down: The Art of Spiritual Restoration

Common Sense for Men and Women in Ministry

A Book of Common Power: Narratives Against the Current

Superwoman Turns Forty

REVEREND DONNA SCHAPER

GRASS ROOTS
GARDENING
RITUALS FOR SUSTAINING ACTIVISM

NATION BOOKS
NEW YORK

GRASSROOTS GARDENING:
Rituals for Sustaining Activism

Copyright © Donna Schaper 2007

Published by
Nation Books
An Imprint of Avalon Publishing Group, Inc.
245 West 17th Street, 11th Floor
New York, NY 10011
www.nationbooks.org

Nation Books is a copublishing venture of the Nation Institute
and Avalon Publishing Group, Incorporated.

Sections of this manuscript appeared in
Teaching My Daughter to Mulch, Ashgrove Press, 1995.

Library of Congress Cataloging-in-Publication Data

ISBN-10: 1-56858-345-1
ISBN-13: 978-1-56858-345-7

9 8 7 6 5 4 3 2 1

Book design by Pauline Neuwirth, Neuwirth & Associates, Inc.

Printed in Canada
Distributed by Publishers Group West

To my brother Jesse Osterhoudt,
who runs a just landscape business in
Raleigh, North Carolina

CONTENTS

GRASS ROOTS

GARDENING

PREFACE

SEASONALITY:
THE RITUAL OF CHANGE

GARDENING IS OFTEN associated with conservatives. By conservatives I mean people who
stay put on either land or ideas, people who
conserve what is good about the past and about their
surroundings. But gardening can also be a progressive
act, a useful activity for those who don't stay put on
either land or ideas. Gardeners can have their mojo on
or off, both, not either. We can be motion people or
stationary people, and we can grow things *both* ways.
Here I show how people who prefer future to past,
motion to stability, and flexibility to rigidity can be
good gardeners while also showing how gardening
helps people with dynamite in their pants to change
the world: it sustains us as we prod the world along.

The book is a how-to for activists and gardeners:
how to grow gardens and how to grow social change,

while staying sane. It is also a bit of a memoir, by accident, showing how gardens grew in the many places where I have been an activist minister. While starting soup kitchens and shelters, community gardens, community organizations, immigration rights campaigns, farm workers' campaigns, pro-choice organizing, FTAA protests, Global Debt reduction efforts, and so on, I have been an active gardener. The gardens have been my source of inspiration, meditation, and mojo.

Long ago I stopped using the words "liberal" and "conservative" because they didn't describe most of the people I know. Instead I started using "open" and "closed" to describe both my red and blue friends. I have many closed liberal friends and many open conservative friends as well as a lot of closed conservative "friends" and open liberal friends. Gardening opens—and therefore is a good ritual for activists. In gardening I open, aerate, fertilize, grow, and change. I like to defy definition by expanding it. I am both a progressive political and a half-decent gardener. I love land and place and old stone foundations. Here I explain how gardening is a ritual that sustains activists like me. I show how soil can save soul by keeping us open to surprise and serendipity. I make fun of activists who don't know how to have fun and like to keep the earnestness of my political tribe at arm's length.

I am the granddaughter of an afternoons-only upstate strawberry and potato farmer. In the morning my grandfather did the rural mail route. He sold our land for an elementary school in Uptown Kingston, New York. I sometimes still go to look at this old land on which I enjoyed many long afternoons. What I remember most is the way warm went to chill as day deepened into night. This book is about change as life's centrifugal force, about moving and returning, which is part of the bridge that can be built between liberals and conservatives. One of the ways we stay open and refuse the stuffiness and inertness of some dirt is to touch soil with the intention of keeping it fertile—what I call gardening. We gardeners push dirt around.

My family moved a lot after we left Kingston when I was eleven. We lived in Saluda, Camden, and Orangeburg, South Carolina. We also lived in Martinsburg, West Virginia, where I graduated from high school. I didn't garden as a girl, but I did eat Mrs. Small's beefsteak tomatoes on King Street in Martinsburg. I became reacquainted to gardening after I graduated from divinity school, when I was living in a hippie commune outside of Gettysburg, Pennsylvania. That garden was not MINE but OURS—and it was a mess, even though it (somehow) fed us. From then on I gardened in lots of places and continued the family pattern of moving. There were stints in Tucson, Philadelphia, Chicago, and back to Gettysburg—then I settled down into my first real adult garden. The previous stints were all rehearsals. The play opened in Riverhead, New York.

Working as a minister moved me into that mobile world of military brats and garment industry foremen. My family of origin moved because my father trained black women throughout the South in how to run sewing machines, as the garment industry fled the unionized North. I married a man whose father was in the Navy—having moved a lot while married and raising our three kids. Although our family was not together in all these places—Arizona, Philadelphia, Chicago, and Amherst, Massachusetts, twice, Riverhead, New York, Miami, Florida, and now Manhattan—these are all places where I have made gardens and pastored activist churches. The story I tell here is about those gardens and about the rituals that sustained my activist ministry. They are linked by place followed by placelessness, which is the metaphor for my life and gardens. The first part of the book is about real places; the second part of the book is about gardening anywhere.

While I used to HATE moving, especially as a girl, I have now come to love it. I have learned how to feed an insatiable appetite for the new, while remaining grounded. Gardens have been the ground, which has rooted me as a citizen of the globe. I have loved all kinds of dirt in all kinds of places, and in each place I have improved the soil.

When you are as gypsy a gardener as I am, you sometimes have to explain yourself. Sustaining rituals about the new and growing is its own paradox. Why sustain? Why new? Why sustain the capacity for the new? Because too much "old" means you are stuck in a past where too few people have the power the many need. And too much new means you are floating on the surface and don't see how many bones are buried just beneath the soil. Gardening is a landed, dirty ritual that sustains hope for the new—which is another way of saying gardens sustain activists.

Let me introduce Frank, who is another bridge between the open and the closed worlds we all inhabit. I see him just about every day when I walk my dog at Stuyvesant Park in New York City. He sits in the same place. The day after Daylight Savings Time arrived and I saw Frank, I noticed he was shivering because the sun had changed and was no longer lighting his bench at 8 a.m. I said, "Frank, you are shivering. Move over to the bench in the sun." "No," he said with more vigor than you would expect from an eighty-year-old homeless man. "This is my bench."

Before you make too much fun of Frank's cold rigidity, hear my thesis. Life is seasonal, which is to say, it shifts, the sun shifts, the moon shifts, time shifts. You pick strawberries until the sun goes down and the chill comes in. Daylight is saved and then spent. But we don't necessarily enjoy the same seasonality as human beings. In fact, many people resist political hope because they would rather shiver in the cold. As one politician describes the rest of us, "We are in a giant car heading towards a brick wall and

everyone is arguing over where they are going to sit."
As a gardener, I have a front-row seat on global warming and the many other idiocies of capitalism
untamed. Humanity is headed for a brick wall of
inequality and injustice that breeds war and destroys
the air. I believe we can change; that is what makes
me an activist. I garden to remind myself of my hope.

Some gardeners go "all the way" back to the farm.
I don't. I garden from an urban viewpoint. I garden in
what I think of as a forward-to-nature rather than
back-to-nature point of view. I argue here for a gardening in the midst of the city approach, not by its
exit. You may not know Eliot Coleman's magnificent
four-season gardening books The model is important
to respect, if not for all to imitate. Scott and Helen
Nearing, the authors of the pre-eminent off-the-grid
handbook *Living the Good Life*, first drew Coleman to
Harborside, Maine. Scott was an economics professor,
Helen a musician, but this politically active couple
left New York to homestead in Vermont in 1932,
thereby rejecting "a society gripped by depression and
unemployment, falling a prey to fascism, and on the
verge of another world-wide military free-for-all."
(*No!* America?) The Nearings moved to Maine in
1952 to convert another derelict New England farm,
Camp Rosier, into a self-sufficient rural community.
In 1968, Coleman, a self-described "semipro adven-
turer" with a graduate degree in Spanish literature,
went to Cape Rosier, as many did, seeking the

Nearings. "They made small farming sound like an adventure," he says. He and his partner now live and farm on part of their property.

Whether it is Helen and Scott Nearing hauling stone for decades to build their "Good Life" house or the deep green Thai garden down the street in New York or the brand new but old-fashioned community-supported agriculture sites that are overbreeding nationally, bringing food from farmers you can name to real people who eat real food, agriculture is recreational hope. It recreates hope. You can recreate hope off the grid or on the grid. I work on the grid. Fun hope is the soil in which serious hope can grow. A lot of people are stuck in (legitimate) despair. Gardening and farming—agricultures—can grow them out of it.

Stuck can feel safe but is usually just the opposite. I know Frank really likes *his bench*. But, you know, it wouldn't kill him to move every now and then.

Seasonality is living well with change. It is motion on behalf of security. It is getting in the last picnic before the summer is over and finding the gloves before you need them. Stuck from a gardener's perspective is death. It is inertness. It is preferring death to life.

I know a formerly great church in Philadelphia that keeps the former pastor's glasses on his desk and his Bible open to the page where he left it when he died thirty-five years ago. No, they have not been able to keep a new pastor: many people prefer museum to motion.

Improvisation is another positive way of talking about seasonality. A friend told me the story of two drummers drumming for a gift on the subway platform. They were seated on the floor. Another man heard the music, and jumped down on the floor and added his guitar. Now, that is music. That is motion. That is seasonality. That is what gardeners do when it looks like the bean crop is going to get eaten by aphids. We improvise—sometimes pouring beer on them can help. Gardeners enact a drama that leaves not one green bean behind, if we can at all help it. That drama extends to children.

Appreciating seasonality allows us to find balance in an off-balance world. The world is dynamic not static; we need each other. We need something to hold on to in order to stay balanced. What happens in an off-balance world is that we keep moving toward false stabilities. False stabilities are another way of saying stuck, dank, and inert. We become cold and rigid. Gardening is an actual and symbolic way to stay nimble and avoid inflexibility.

I stay alive remembering the outreach of an old apple tree and the way it carries an idiosyncratic eloquence. Season by season the weight of its fruit has twisted each individual limb. The tree changes in shape. Embracing seasonality enables us to prepare for the deaths that will come to us and to those we love. Gardeners "get" seasons. Once we get seasons, we are able to understand the many ideas and ideals that surround us.

Another point of view regarding seasonality is E. M. Forster's in *Aspects of the Novel*. Here he understands and explores the futility of contrasting liberals and conservatives.

It is amusing to listen to elderly people on this subject. Sometimes a man says in confident tones, human nature is the same in all ages. The primitive cave man lies deep within us all. . . . He speaks like this when he is feeling prosperous and fat. When he is feeling depressed and worried by the young, or is being sentimental about them on the ground that they will succeed in life when he has failed, then he will take the opposite view and say mysteriously, human nature is not the same, I have seen fundamental changes in my own time. You must face facts . . . and he goes on like this day after day, alternately facing facts and refusing to alter them.

You may think a garden an odd place to have this kind of philosophical conversation, about whether things can change or not. I think it is the absolute right, not wrong, place to have such a conversation. I want to explain the possibility and hope that grounds many others and me. It is not an accident that the World Social Forum slogan is "Another world is possible." My hope is this: If human nature does alter it will be because individuals manage to look at themselves in a new way. Here and there people are trying to do just that, and every institution and vested interest is against this search. This is why we must look to novels and dirt to save us. E. M. Forster understood how the novel is revolutionary, in the same way that I see the garden as revolutionary.

> . . . If the novelist sees himself differently he will see his characters differently and a new system of lighting will result. So in a crablike way . . . the development of the novel might mean the development of humanity.

Gardens teach us to see ourselves differently. Gardens allow us to see ourselves in crablike growth and crablike failure to grow. Gardens take hoeing humanity to parabolic levels. If social change does not result, often snow peas do. Thinking of ourselves as people who grow a mean snow pea grounds hope in more beautiful and nourishing greenings.

Note to Reader: Because the garden is a constantly changing stability and because its tense is both past, present, and future, you will note that these essays are dated. Resist being confused by tenses. Resist my nightmare of not really knowing which town or city I now live in or whether you can grow arugula there in November. Instead, enjoy the permanence of the impermanent nature of gardening.

· PART ONE ·

GARDENING AND PLACE

NEVER DESERT GARDENING

THE RITUAL OF THE NEIGHBORHOOD

Tucson, Arizona 1973–1975

 I ONLY GARDENED in Arizona for two years, but while there I learned an important lesson. You can garden anywhere. I repeat: One can garden anywhere. Lots of people think the desert is hostile to growth because it is too hot and too dry. That is not true. Both conditions can be successfully overcome.

Those of you who are native plants fundamentalists will not like what follows. You will want northerners who go west or south to adapt to what grows there already. You will not understand how good our tomatoes were in Pennsylvania from which we came. You will not understand the passion to reproduce them in Arizona. You may even think of Northern transplants to the desert as immoral or imperialist. Why live here if you really live there in your head?

We amended the desert soil in order to get that tomato taste. We took one look at that empty lot next door to our little crumbling Spanish home on Second Avenue in downtown Tucson in the early seventies and saw garden. Yes, the garbage had to be removed. And, of course, the neighbors had to be organized. We knew how much garbage they had. We knew they would bring it to us. And they did. Our major problem was to get them to stop bringing their table scraps once they started. People would ring the doorbell at midnight and hope that we weren't asleep, so that we could put their dinner leavings into the compost heap. Yes, we removed the meat that erroneously accompanied some people. Yes, we rejected the grass clippings from yards that were just too damn green: we knew the amount of chemicals they contained and didn't see a thing those chemicals would do for our garden. And yes, we had enormous failures: like the day it rained (which it almost never does) and ruined all the strawberries. Just wiped them out. They were doing fine with the "gray" water we were carrying from the house. Deluge was not their delight.

Linda Rondstadt lived across the street, but the neighborhood was mostly Hispanic. She never participated in the neighborhood garbage gathering. She may have been in the barrio but was certainly not of the barrio, plus she was almost never home. Still, before our great garden, the only thing people could say about the neighborhood was that Linda Ronstadt sort of lives here.

The local gangs actually defended the garden rather than trashing it. Why? "Those tomatoes are pretty good and they'll give you all you want. Why steal 'me'?"

I was once in South Africa with a community organizer. She took me to a place she said was a beautiful lake. She showed me all its secrets and described the nature of its blue color. I saw nothing. She kept saying, look deeper. I did and realized I was looking at her dream, not her reality. She was trying to get irrigation and local water. After several more years of touring pilgrims through her desert she did. Visualizing the lake was a part of her campaign.

We did nothing so profound in Tucson. Several dozen tomato plants worked really great, and we had two seasons per year, fall and winter. Lettuce never. Cucumbers never. Corn never. Strawberries were magnificent in the one season when conditions were right for them. What we learned was the lesson about the permanent possibility of gardens.

The practical way we encouraged others' involvement was not just through the neighborhood burnt offerings. We also organized the youth group at the First Congregational Church. We taught the youth group how to grow compost in the church parking lot. We sold it as "Holy ——" for a dollar a bag and had all the old ladies in the church bring us their kitchen scraps. We added grass clippings and other ingredients and made $3000 in one year selling our excellent compost. The youth group took that money on an "urban plunge" to San Francisco, where we stayed in shelters and ate in soup kitchens and had an awfully educational fight on the last night of the trip about what to do with our surplus money. Should we give it to one of the soup kitchens or take ourselves out to the top of the Marc? We did both. During that trip we also watched the San Francisco police department "accept" women cops. The issue was in the paper the morning we visited the downtown precinct. One of our students was a strong horsewoman. The cop giving us the tour told us that the reason women couldn't be cops is they couldn't pass the physical. You had to carry a hundred pounds a hundred feet while walking a straight line. Carol picked up one of the bags that was lying there, carried it two hundred feet, and put it down. We enjoyed just how far Holy —— can go.

I also loved watching the ladies come to church, wearing hats and carrying plastic bags proudly next to their purses. Double wrapped usually, recycled, and containing the daintiest of carrot peels and lettuce outers. I loved the night the church board of trustees decided it wasn't quite right to have all that manure we had received from a local ranch in the church parking lot—as though manure was somehow unholy. One of the old ladies showed up and argued for the manure, for the compost—and against the waste of her garbage disposal. The motion to close us down failed—and we still had tomatoes that year.

No, the compost in the parking lot did not smell. People were just afraid that it might. The breakdown and heat of the mixture we made—leaves, grass clippings, manure, and table scraps—caused the compost to be made within two weeks. There wasn't time for smell.

There are people who fear you can't garden in the desert. They are wrong. There are people who think women can't carry heavy burdens. They too are wrong.

2

TEACHING MY DAUGHTER TO MULCH

The Ritual of Effort

Riverhead, New York, 1987–1993

I HAVE SAID it before: I plant too much. Each year I add annuals to spots where perennials grow. On top of hollyhock and baby's breath, I drop zinnias or beans. The competition for nourishment begins.

No doubt my daughter feels the same way as my overplanted garden in the competition for nourishment. Her father and I take care not only of her, but her brothers, and the planet, our jobs, and our politics. Her father and I also do windows.

With us the earth had too much to handle. We became heavy, even heavier than it could bear. We should never have reproduced ourselves because there is very little about our biological life that respects either evolution or what we do with our lives. We eat wrong, drive wrong, and most of our backs feel as if we shouldn't even be standing up on such a regular basis.

Our lives are too much for the soil in which they are meant to grow. We are pale green plants, requiring extraordinary amounts of chemical fertilizers. We are biologically immoral, environmentally untenable. I can't imagine why I begin to worry about zinnias or beans or hollyhocks.

But worry I do. I don't want my annuals to crowd my perennials, so I have opened new gardens almost every year. I had a little less than one acre on the eastern tip of Long Island when my daughter was two years old to eight years old. The back of the property descended into swamp, which connects to river, which connects to bay, which connects to ocean. I own only the swamp. All those connections took about seven miles to complete.

My first garden was in the front yard, the second in the back. The third was the in back of the back. Pretty soon I hit swamp, where my genetic repentance and soil-building projects met their match.

I began with sand. Tan Long Island sand. The first year, in the front, I added about thirty one-hundred-pound feedbags of cow manure. The second year we mulched the flimsy soil with grass clippings hauled from the yard of almost every neighbor in a two-square-mile district. I panicked only once: What if some of the neighbors were using chemical weed control? What if I was poisoning my own soil with their clippings? It is the same panic I knew from that year's apple juice scare: What if, in the name of nourishing my children, I had fed them poisoned apple juice? I kept trying to tone down the words *poison* and *panic*. It never worked.

No doubt I did borrow some pollution. But at least I didn't pay for it. I hauled it. I even reused the plastic bags in which my neighbors had packed the makings of my new garden. A semi-annual dose of lime also helped. One year I had some magnificent rotting hay. The mulch was better than normal, breaking down more slowly into a more complex nourishment. It might have been as good as my compost, or the fish carcasses that slowly rotted below the tomato plants.

I also took my neighbors' leaves. Each autumn we hauled about two hundred bags of leaves, first to the front, then after another century to the back. The decomposition of the lime and the manure and the leaves and the grass clippings gave us space to plant more than we could possibly maintain. Am I proud of all this hard work and the back that made it possible? You bet. When I'm not humiliated, that is. The whole process was such a perfect example of the repentance of which I am capable: two steps backward, one forward, in that great march toward oblivion that my species is making.

First, I recover *useless* soil by improving it. I march back to a sustainable time. Then, instead of being satisfied with a little, I march forward a lot. I overextend and overplant in complete imitation of the human species' general habit. This one step forward requires more mulch to keep the maintenance low. So far, so good. Neither gods nor genes have rejected my liturgical march back to the swamp, even twenty years later.

Mulch makes my confession. I couldn't possibly weed all plots once they are in and growing. Also, I needed the annual improvement of the decaying mulch. Furthermore, watering this leaky, sandy stuff cost the larger environment and me too much. In the name of all these sensibilities, I have to get mulch down pretty quickly after the garden is planted. Not too soon, of course, since the soil has to warm. The end of May was usually ideal for the mulching.

One year we shook hands with the ideal time before it eluded us. That near miss is the origin of this long defense of the size of my garden. The idea that I could be happy with two yellow marigolds and a zinnia in a box or a bucket of geraniums and a row of beans is insulting. I don't like the ordinary garden, and I don't like small gardens. God has tapped my shoulder. Maybe the garden is not really overextended. I just know the tyranny of growth so well that I begin to fear it everywhere. I begin to wonder if I can leave anything alone.

Comfortable white Americans like me plant gardens that are too big. With us, it's a way of life. God forbid I should be satisfied with a normal eight-hour life. I work too long at my job, and I work too hard at my garden. I have other excesses, but there is no point in going into them right now.

Anyway, my back didn't go out until after I had shaken hands with the ideal. I saw its face; I knew what it would mean to befriend it. We were in the third year of this particular project. It happened in almost the same casual way that the earth could self-destruct. The spring had been extraordinarily wet. I had two gardens to get in, and the third needed a good weeding. We had come to the end of May, and, behold, the sun came out on a Saturday. I was going to get in the gardens in and the mulch down unless it killed me.

Which, of course, it nearly did. I dug and dug and kneeled and kneeled and then dug some more and kneeled some more. All of a sudden I felt a feeling I had never experienced before. My back wouldn't get straight. I couldn't figure out if it was the earth that said no or my body that said no, but definitely the great refusal to carry on had begun. Of course I paid no attention to the warning. I kept digging and kneeling and getting up and down to dig and kneel some more. I dared the garden to kill me.

Which it nearly did.

The dare-to-kill attitude is probably the same attitude that got us worrying about whose flag to put on the moon. Surely the dinosaurs, as brains got dispro-portionate to brawn, would have driven cars with the same going-to-get-there-if-it-kills-me attitude that the early twenty-first century values so highly. Going fast is part of overextending. If we don't go fast, we don't really have time to do so much. If we don't do so much, then we resign our citizenship in the upper crust. Part of being the upper crust is to go fast enough to use more than our share. The speed and the direction are a lethal combination.

On the same day that my back went out, I had intended to teach my daughter to mulch. She would be my salvation because with her labor added to my labor, theoretically, we could *get more done*.

My daughter mulched differently than I. I, in the interest of my citizenship, carried as much as I possibly could and carried it as swiftly as I possibly could to its destination. She, in the service of some five-year-old muse, picks up small hands of grass clippings and, like a fairy princess dusting with stardust, places a few of the clippings gently on the head of a Montauk Daisy. She then walks the five hundred feet back to the clipping pile, picks up another handful of grass clippings and, muttering magical incantations, dusts a day lily or pea pod. She says she is going to start on the raspberries tomorrow, a project that should take her several hundred years.

I want to retrieve soil from swamp and sand ASAP. I don't know how much longer we'll live here; I don't have time to waste; and I don't think I'll be happy with just three gardens. I have too many projects, too many plans. Like the nation of my birth, I have a mission in

this garden. My mission is to improve it. I am a veri-
table machine out there.

A few days post-back and post-chiropractic, I told
Katie about my plans to teach her fast gardening. She
objected on several counts to the curriculum. She didn't
want to hurt her back the way I had hurt mine.
Therefore she had no intention of overdoing it. She
didn't want to rush because rushing got in the way of
skipping. She refused the lesson in efficient mulching
on the grounds of avoiding pain and having fun. Then
she got distracted and skipped away, empty-handed.
In the twinkle of an eye, I was alone again in the back
garden, mulching away by myself. Katie was deep in
the swamp, lifting stones and looking for mealy bugs.
She was singing some song I couldn't quite hear.
Usually these days it's Peter Pan's rendition of "I don't
want to grow up."

How exactly am I supposed to teach this child to
mulch or, better yet, to grow up? I wish I could con-
clude that her ways are better, but I can't. Children
are not the solution to the problem adults have made.
Fairy dust would never have tamed the prairies. No
matter how much of an environmental romantic I have
become, I'm pretty sure somebody had to figure out
how to grow enough grain to feed all the people that
we have overplanted.

If there is a culprit, it is my childlike ignorance of
limits. I don't know how to stop. It's almost as if I
need someone to stop me. Wait till I tell Katie it's

dark and it's time for her to go to bed. She won't want to hear a word of it, and it won't be because she is an American, but rather that she is a child. I'll have to carry her kicking and screaming all the way from the rear garden into the house.

Mulch will be the trick I'll teach her because I don't really quite believe in nature. I think we can improve on nature, that we can make it come alive again with living things. Sand grows no spinach. More troubling is the matter of how much spinach we need.

The trick will be teaching my little Peter Pan how to improve the soil without breaking her back, my back, or the earth's back. The farmer in me can't let her think that she can live on the soil effortlessly. The environmentalist in me can't let her think that all soil needs her improvement. My job is to teach Katie what I don't yet know. It is yet another repentance isn't it, to raise our children better than we were raised ourselves?

To spoil soil as a way to improving it? To go just one step forward and one step back to a better future? Or, in the telling of these stories, to march forward to a better past?

3

PULLING UP ROOTS

THE RITUAL OF OWNERSHIP

Moving from Riverhead to Amherst, 1993

MOVING A GARDEN is a lot easier than most people think. The reason is that gardening is about the garden—and it is the gardener who moves, not the soil. Just last night my husband wanted to know if I wanted to bother planting the soup's fish heads in next year's tomato spot. Did I want to bother, since we are moving in a matter of weeks? Of course I wanted to bother. Somebody will till the soil if not me. I may be moving my garden, but I am not moving *the* garden. Garden is means, not end; process, not product; spiritual not physical. Spiritual processes are light as a feather. You just pick them up and bring them with you.

My daughter accuses me of only wanting to move to the new house on West Street in Amherst because of the garden. (She prefers the place on Bay Road with the horse barn and the above-ground pool.) She is absolutely right. I took one look at the ancient English cottage garden west of the house and said I'd take the place. I was not swayed in the original judgment by the appearance of asbestos on the boiler or red velvet wallpaper in the living room. The garden would save me years. For the first time in years I wouldn't have to build one from scratch. I could build on someone else's beginning.

I say this with respect for that part of gardening that is backbreaking work, which is end, product, and physical. You can do something about each of these matters if you have the other skills. The other skills are the courage and the heart to garden. They are spiritual skills, maybe even lusts. They carry the weight.

I know about this ease with which gardens move because I have moved so many. Tucson moved to Pennsylvania. And Tucson was a city garden with desert earth. It was a tough garden, but it still produced strawberries—the second year. Pennsylvania was a comparatively easy garden. It was built on an ancient ruin. The weeds grew as well as the plants. Southeastern Pennsylvania moved to Philadelphia, which moved to New Haven, which moved to Amherst, which moved to Chicago, which moved to the eastern end of Long Island, which is now moving back to Amherst. I was in Chicago twice; one time as a student and then I didn't think I needed to garden. Persephone and I like to return.

I have never stayed long enough for the asparagus to come up. Still, except for Tucson, Philadelphia, and Chicago—where space was at a premium—I planted asparagus. The only thing I regret is the expense. It comforts me to know that someone else has what might have been considered my asparagus.

I created a mythological plant, named Ruby Begonia, who is sort of a whore. She follows me everywhere and makes her living on the street. Otherwise when I kiss a garden good-bye, it is gone. I expect no followers and don't usually even take cuttings or bulbs. That modest form of theft I reserve for other people's gardens. After all, I have given two other people a lot of asparagus: why shouldn't I reap a bulb or two?

Once you have the courage and the heart to garden, moving is easy. Understanding that gardening is a low-cost form of personal entertainment allows moving to be light. Moving doesn't mean you stop going to the movies; therefore it shouldn't mean that you stop gardening. Lightness always moves easy.

The gypsy in me appreciates at least three things about gardens: their lightness, the importance of the natural redistribution of things (which some see as stealing), and the entertainment.

First the lightness. We usually buy our houses for the gardens and not the houses. (Which may be one reason we were so miserable in those 900 indoor square feet in Riverhead for six years.) The gardening impulse bought this house on the eastern end of Long Island. What was here was land and forest. We had to clear the half-acre of forest before we could even start the garden. The congregation of the church here had the same opposite-of-effortless feeling—and that's another reason to leave them and try another. I haven't told the kids that yet. They'll find out soon enough that some people don't want to bloom, process or no process.

The way to clear a half-acre of forest is to put up a sign in your front yard that says "free wood." The men who are married to the women who clip coupons show up with chain saws. Granted, they leave unsightly stumps, but vines hide them well. Plus, in a flat land, a little elevation helps.

Once the forest is cleared, especially if it is this close to the sea, the sand needs to be built up. Mild winters make it possible to do this in almost two years granting, of course, that no one has raked leaves on the property for a decade. After that, the only real cost is the lime. The lightness of gardening is not only spiritual; it is also directly proportional to how many other people are doing the heavy work. The wonderful part about this community was the way people helped each other, bloom or no bloom. I always felt they just didn't have enough light.

Similar principles apply to the redistribution of garden wealth. If you want to own your asparagus, then you will feel too attached to it. If you want to own your labor, it will become too heavy. The heaviness will come from the attachment. Giving it away as you grow it—whether the gift be wood or asparagus or your labor when next door wants to be clear—keeps the heaviness of ownership from invading the entertainment of gardening. And the entertainment will never be as expensive as the movies.

Pulling up a garden is easy once we understand what gardens are. They are light, inexpensive forms of entertainment. They don't move; we move.

Our efforts have resulted in soil worth planting in. Our soil granted thirteen kinds of Italian lettuce last year as well as over one hundred red raspberry bushes in maturity. (The raspberry bushes came courtesy of two families in the congregation who did know how to grow.) The asparagus is still, after all this time, discontented with its lot. It will come. The strawberries look good but they don't produce enough. I think lime may have been overdone in their neighborhood. The Chinese green beans loved it in that location. (Location, location, location say the real estate people.) Sweet peas never grew here either, but I have a feeling that they will some year. Not just born of my own optimism, this is an educated feeling. I know they are heavy eaters, but really! I have given them enough already. One year I had an entire rabbit hutch of rabbit waste. I think it will work.

The snow peas couldn't have done better but basil hated its place in the rotation this year, and its failure particularly bothered me as my dear friend in Massachusetts reported growing three new kinds.

And on and on, with that series of successes and failures, jealousies and victories, that making a garden implies. Lightness toward the failures helps; otherwise you can get really bogged down.

The front yard was an even better example of this repetition of fun and failure. Because there wasn't enough sun the first year, even after the forest was cleared in the back due to the neighbors' not wanting to give away any free wood—we plowed up the front yard. It became easy to tell people which place was ours, "The only one on the street with the garden in front." The neighbor who was not going to like us anyway flipped out and called central zoning only to be told that you can do whatever you want with your front yard. He also called about the goats, the chickens, and the rabbits in the back yard and was told the same thing.

The front yard had its origin in conflict. When we put about a dozen bags of rather chunky cow manure into the plowed-up front garden, he was apoplectic. "You have a lot of %$#& in your front yard." I renewed my prayer that when I retired I would have more to do than pick up each leaf as it dropped on my zoysia grass. It had not helped that the one time the dog got out she pooped on his zoysia grass. Of all the people in the neighborhood on whose property she might have pooped! The children developed an enemy out of it anyway, and every child needs one genuine enemy. He fit the bill perfectly.

In the front yard, because of the sun and the heavy manure, the garden took off the first year. I brought in the expensive peonies from the high-rent nursery in Litchfield, Connecticut. By the second year they were magnificent. We didn't have any other place to put the pear trees we had been given for an earlier Christmas, so we just stuck them in there too. They are now so big they look kind of ridiculous. I am thinking of pulling them up and taking them to Massachusetts, although I have a terrible feeling that the tree, which is doing well in this mild a winter, won't do so well where the winter is a more serious opponent to personal and agricultural warmth.

The mums I collected from several states gave good old burnt-orange a real run for its money. And they came up every year. But the real runaway victory in the front garden has been the love affair between the cosmos and the morning glory. Three years now we haven't been able to plant a thing, so joyous have they been in their arrangement. Bloom, bloom, bloom. The glories climb the pear trees that makes for a bit of a hodgepodge. But now that we have picked up every stakelike thing within five miles, you should see their ostentation. And I do try to keep them off the pear trees.

Obviously, the climate and the cows and the free-wood people kept the process light here. So did the stealing, which I prefer to see as redistribution. The moral basis is here: if I leave asparagus all over the country, why shouldn't I pick up what other people leave behind when I move?

People see our old green Volvo station wagon coming, and they add to their recycling piles. Recycling is one of the more sophisticated ways to redistribute the wealth. People know we can probably use some of what they have put out. The stakes have been a real delight to find. I even found some pretty wrought iron ones that were actually meant for use in the garden. The rest are dead brooms and the like.

The back yard suffers, some of our friends tell us, from our penchant for recycling. Two of our closest friends have actually told us that we'd better "do something about it" if we want to sell the house before we move. And God knows, we want to sell the house before we move. We bought this four-bedroom, four-bath Cape at the height of the Long Island real estate boon for $140,000 and then the market crashed. One-third of my congregation was unemployed. Our friends, who are more suburban in their point of view, think the property won't sell until we cover the compost pile, remove the goats, rabbits, and chickens, take out the huge tire and dead tractor the kids play on, etc., etc. I'd as soon kill my mother.

What they don't know is that the first ad I put in the local paper, "In-town organic farmette on one acre near forest preserve, for sale for a lot less than it should or did cost," drew dozens of inquiries. None of the people had any money, but still there is a market for a place with this much already planted. Even in Riverhead, which would like to think it is long past its organic roots but isn't.

From my point of view this property is nothing if not a steal. Or a redistribution of wealth.

You should meet the people who came to look at the house. Five Ukrainian immigrants, one a medical doctor working as an orderly at the local hospital; a Baptist Evangelist and his wife who didn't think the basement was big enough for services; two group homes for retarded children; and at least a dozen single mothers with that many children each, it seemed. So far not one of them has been the slightest bit daunted by the size of the garden.

We did have one family of European background with two kids, who looked a lot like we do, show up. They were gone in a flash. They even had the money for the rent.

Before we pull up, somebody will show up who likes the garden and has enough money to pay what we owe the bank each month. One thousand dollars. Per month! Now that is what I call stealing. Heavy handed, not entertaining stealing. At least we have the garden and can take it with us. Lightly redistributing wealth is a good description of gardening.

That this garden has sneaked in between forest and house so easily will make it a particularly hard one to leave. But it belongs here and I don't anymore. It is almost out of respect for each other that we part.

Our place will someday sell to just the right person because it is too idiosyncratic to sell to the wrong person. The recession can only heighten its value over time. Like walking, sex, and reading, gardening costs only the labor of appearing. Someone on the hunt for that kind of bargain will soon appear. (Or we'll rent it to a half dozen Ukrainian immigrants.)

The third leg of the lightness is the entertainment. If the first is the way spiritual resources create partnerships in which they outweigh physical difficulties and the second is socialist, the redistribution of wealth, then the third is surely the low-cost form of entertainment.

Gardening differs slightly from the simpler forms of cheap fun. You can find lots of ways to spend money on the garden. In January and February the seductions abound. I did fantasy seed buying the other night and managed to total a $200 seed and nursery order. It was the new roses and the astilbes that did it, although that many campanulas are bound to add up. I won't send all these orders, but it was fun to let my credit card enjoy itself for the evening. Even if we are moving, I still like to spend my winter evenings this way.

When we left Arizona, I did winter buying after figuring out how to grow flowers in the downtown desert there. (Recycle water.) I still ordered seeds the winter we moved back to the farm in Pennsylvania and the winter we moved to Chicago. In both places, the first because we had no money and the second because we had no land, the gardening was really about the same as it has been here—more mental than physical. More a low-cost form of personal entertainment than a thing that actually had to happen. Even though we have produced an actual garden here, the pleasure has been mostly spiritual.

The spiritual fun of it consists in the practical challenge: how to keep the entertainment low cost and personal. I have discovered at least two practical ways to keep the costs down and the fun up in the garden. One is the idea of a bulb bash.

Apparently this idea has been as widely circulated as its barn-raising predecessor. I, who previously thought I had considered every way to survive without money, having bartered a funeral for a will from a lawyer, baptisms for tulip bulbs, and weddings for sauerkraut made the right way, community organizing for red raspberries, etc., was astonished to be informed of the bulb bash. Simply, you have a party in which everyone brings and plants a bulb or perennial. Your garden grows because your friends have extra of this or that. You spend the time normally used for cocktails in directing friends to previously dug, composted holes. They plant their offerings. From then on your tulips remind you of Susan, the phlox of Norman, the peach tree of Gene. Personalized, without those awful delivery charges at the end of nursery orders, planted—how much more thrifty can you get? And, starting the cocktail hour later is no sin.

Early spring or late fall parties can be had in the same year. The only warning is not to return peaches to Gene (he doesn't need them) or tell Susan you don't like that color there. Feelings are fragile. When your friends have their bulb bash, you need to bring something new. You might eventually need one of those books that old-fashioned hostesses used to record party details in—broccoli divan when the Chesterfields were here in 1972—just to make sure you don't serve it if they come again.

Another way to keep the gardening costs down and the diversity high is to steal perennials. There is no point in obfuscation. During most of the growing season here, I wear the pants with the big pockets for my walks. Seed catching has made my wildflower patch a real dream. I find the strongest flowers in the field and steal their seeds. They don't mind. They are glad to be useful, to be fruitful, and to multiply.

I have been caught on country roadsides with a shovel, digging up daylilies that had a good bright or raspberries that were overgrown. The people who catch me usually pull out their own shovel or consent to let mine do the work for them. These roadside galas are too infrequently pruned. They need me to help them prepare for next year's show. I would never touch a plant or even a seed with a house close by. I would never take a whole plant, only its excess. I always mark the asparagus in the fall when they sprout their Christmas tree balls on their ferns. That way I can find them in the spring when they show up and not insult them by letting their work get big and hard and fall over, unnoticed and unappreciated. I can get two good meals of asparagus if I can take the time to make the hour-long drive it takes to gather all the rosebuds while I may. Obviously this is comfort for my asparagus failures in the area at home.

The abandoned doctors' offices in the middle of our ugly strip of malls provided me enough fresh roses for the entire month of June. I waited one full year before picking them and watched as they slowly went bad. I felt that I should get out my shovel and bring these orphans home, but that is close to the negative aspects of stealing. If, in one more year, no one takes over that office, I may have to move those roses to Massachusetts. They need fertilizer. They will die on the new owner on their own, if I do not intervene.

Developers knocked over an old nursery, The Bittersweet, near this same mall strip. They're building a huge grocery store on the spot. The nursery left behind hundreds of large planters, dozens of trellises, lots of dried-up bulbs, and about 200 unsold Christmas trees from their last season. Our outdoor fireplace enjoyed some of their Christmas trees; I made half the bulbs grow; the trellises go great with the dead brooms; and I have given away dozens of large planters. I picked the pumpkin off the vine that was just sitting there in the middle of the field before progress arrived. I am pretty sure I had comrades in this liberation of the useful from the debris; I could tell that somebody took some of the desiccated herbs that I had rejected. I'll bet they made them grow too.

One day I was driving past the spot and The Bittersweet was gone. It had disappeared. It was flat, brown dirt, with evidence of progress's tire marks everywhere in steamroller feet. I wished I had taken all the Christmas trees because they made a great bonfire. We burned our last at New Year's Eve on the stroke of midnight. I consoled myself with having done the best I could and immediately went to one of my forbidden raspberry patches to do some pruning for next year. It was the act of a mother who comes home from taking one of her children to the hospital with a broken leg and spends the rest of the night rocking the other one in the chair. Loss makes you tender.

I have spotted abandoned lupines on a road in Vermont, literally hundreds and hundreds of lupines, right next to a stream. I lust after them. But probably making the trip to Vermont would cost as much as ordering the few I would take. Plus my soil here doesn't have the wet feet in a sunny enough place for the lupines to grow. You know where I'll be late next summer.

Stealing does have limits. Gardening cheaply, however, does not. Pulling up roots would hurt too much if you thought you couldn't make another garden. Because you know you can, it's a bittersweet grief. One day you just wake up and realize that the Riverhead garden is gone. New Year's is on its way.

Some might even call the whole process progress. I prefer the notion of return. A return to the spiritual fun of the garden, only this time in a new soil.

4

FALL CRAYONS

THE RITUAL OF SAYING GOOD-BYE

IN THE FIELD slated for development on Route 58, in Riverhead, the competitions between the colors are in full swing. The wine berries have invited the antique bottles over for a deep blue competition. The mustards and golden-rods have been bickering since breakfast about the relative merits of relative yellows. The purple asters have only the weary phlox left as rivals. The sumac has once again beaten the ivy in turning red, just as the pump-kins close in on an orange for mastery of color.

The greens are out of it, their season being spring and this being very much not that. Spring is small and budding, gentle and pastel, incremental, rising, on its way up. This, fall, is big and baggy, harsh and bright, drooping when not dropping, on its way nowhere, just back home and arriving there sooner than anyone thought it would. The colors quarrel, then settle their arguments. Some wisely know they are in their final season and savor their transformations while others, too young to really understand autumn, show off as if there were no tomorrow. They make fun of the dusty leaves in the way they recklessly yield themselves to every wind. The more sage protect themselves from buffeting, preferring stillness if possible.

The human, immune from the wilds off Route 58 and their noisy pigmentation, are also deep in conversation. They too are talking about fall but the language is muted. Its colors range the hazy spectrum of loss. Maybe this is the last day for a bike ride at the proper temperature, which experts have declared to be seventy-five. Maybe the sheets will have to go in the dryer. I know it's going to be an early frost, I just know it. Gone are shirtsleeves. Gone is sunshine. The squirrels hide their harvest, the humans fill up their Ball jars, otherwise all of summer is lost.

One of the humans is sure to mention the oddity of mourning such a summer. They'll mention the rains, the length and duration of the record-breaking rains, the unbearable humidity. They will compete over mildew. Or they will complain about the heat. Neither the human nor the summer was all it hoped to be.

This conversation is also slated for development. It will develop into next summer, sure to be dry and cool, in a record-breaking sort of way. It will also pass on before its time.

The large scale that we stole from the old farm before it became K-Mart will go to the Amherst backyard. We will surround it with new stones—and use it as an outdoor fireplace. There we will tell the story of how it hung in the old barn, there we will tell how we came to know it was a Long Island duck scale. There we will light fires in our new home, fires from our old home. There we will prepare to say other good-byes.

5

PULLING UP AND PLOTTING THE GARDEN

RITUALS OF THE FALL

Amherst, Massachusetts, 1992–Present, Off and On.

THINKING ABOUT WHAT the garden will be is more fun than the garden's being. Early winter while the ground is still warm through its long summer basking, and before the first snow flies, right before the turkey is cooked, is one of the great times for the gypsy gardener. Gypsy gardeners are the ones who love to move things.

Almost everything will tolerate a move in the northern fall. My mums love long division in this season, as do the day lilies. They wonder how their colors will mix for a long time before they actually do so.

When the writer E. B. White (author of *Charlotte's Web* and many other works) wrote about his wife, Katharine S. White, the author of the famous *Onward and Upward in the Garden*, he remembered her placing bulbs in the ground every autumn, "calmly plotting the resurrection." He wrote these words in the introduction to the eleventh issue of her famous gardening book:

"As the years went by and age overtook her, there was something comical yet touching in her bedraggled appearance on this awesome occasion—the small, hunched-over figure, her studied absorption in the implausible notion that there would be yet another spring, oblivious to the ending of her own days which she knew perfectly well was near at hand, sitting there with her detailed chart under those dark skies in the dying October, calmly plotting the resurrection."

White was more than right about the nature of pleasure. It is something we steal from the darker days for the lighter days. Autumn gardeners are wrong to only focus on the bulbs. There is more to do than just plant. Evaluation and wandering about are also very good November tasks. See who is there. Examine what happened.

I liken this task to that of the women at the grave in the New Testament who confuse Jesus with the gardener. Now you see the flower of your faith; now you don't. Even the big resurrections are off-season in a parabolic way: they happen much too quickly. Then, before and after, even for years to come, we harvest their meanings. Just as we plan in the fall for happening in the spring, we remember in the winters of our days, the messages of the previous springs. At dusk we again hear the sounds of birdsong.

One November I was madly searching for something to do in the garden. I like to do a little piece of its labor every day and to think about what I might do with my few brief moments all day long. It is the same plotting, plotting, dragged out, enjoyed, strategized, and then done. On this day, I said, "I will move the worms." They lived deep in the compost. The compost was hot. I knew of some leaf piles where I had already buried fish heads. By the way, if you have not plotted tomatoes in the early winter by planting fish heads in places pre-destined, do so. It works. The tomatoes love the calcium (or something) about the fish. This early winter day I knew I could still dig the ground. I loved the idea of the worms pulling up their down blanket of snow and snuggling in. So I dug cruelly into the compost and halved a few dozen worms in my clumsy forklift. I put the worms under the leaves, with the fish heads, and dug them in. I actually heard one thank me. They never liked that neighborhood in the first place. The dead were left to bury the dead.

The next spring I had an astonishing number of worms, both in that year's tomato patch and in the old compost. I thought of calling in the Zero Population Growth people to confess my sin. Reproduction in the worm world was clearly out of control.

Another good plot for the winter gardener is to clear brambles. They don't hurt so much when you have on more clothes. As W. S. Merwin puts it in *The Lost Upland* (1993), "the hard brown knots of ancient blackberry kingdoms" love to move. But only if the ground is very friable. They can't penetrate ice crystals.

Hen and chicks in the rock garden will also move around well at this time of year but be sure to cover them with lots of leaves. Keep the leaves of the iris, which will probably have poked through the fall soil if it has been too warm. Be judicious with the leaf blanket though; iris disease loves leaf mold.

Many of us fear, of course, that the garden is more mental plot than actual plot. Someone mean actually said, "What a person thinks of a garden is entirely projection." I forgot his name on purpose. The problem is precisely the opposite. Projecting the garden, mentally, spiritually, emotionally, is gardening. We drag out its meanings through all our parts, through all our seasons. We extend the season this way. Plotting is more like solar tunnels than anything else. It is something we put over the actual ground to let its processes go on longer than they naturally are able to manage.

Gardening, as a whole, is the tension between our projections and our plots. In autumn, we notice what really happened last year. I have to admit that I also moved worms too late one year, and they all died. That death was not a projection.

In the interior garden of the autumnal season, we deal with the reality of what we have seen and the potential failures of our projections. Then, in tension with our hoped-for plot, we plan another garden anyway. Anthony Trollope tells of going down to London on the train with what he thought was a good hand-written manuscript of a long novel. The publisher said, no, thank you. On the train going home, Trollope laid his bulky bundle down on his lap face down and began writing a new book on the back pages of a rejected one. Some of our gardens get rejected by the great publisher as well. We turn them over and begin the story again.

If the beans got disease in the north corner, we should not put them there again. But we can try some other crop in the place where they failed. Plotting is comprehending failure and rising from it, to fail again or maybe even to live.

The great gardener and writer, Vita Sackville-West came to the conclusion that you can't come to a conclusion. Whether to hope in the autumn for a better garden in the spring—or to wait for plotting till the advertisers make their January colonization of the tables next to our chairs—is a serious question. The autumnal plotter will make more conservative choices; the armchair gardener will spend money on behalf of less realistic fantasies.

I cannot explain why some gardens are spectacular and others mediocre and still others spectacular in certain plots and mediocre in others. These displays can change annually also, as we all know. I have failed to grow Italian basil for three years in a row. Then one year they all came up so beautifully that some actually took frost. I couldn't use them all. Christopher Fry, in Part Two of *The Lady's Not For Burning*, says, "I gave you mystery and paradox and what you wanted is cause and effect" (1994). How right he is. Our autumnal walks in the garden are not searches for causes or effects; we are there to visit the mystery and paradox of what lived well and what failed to live well. We are visiting the deathbed of a friend. It is not time to talk about how she smoked too much.

There are those whose grief in the fall is so large that they swear they will not plant another garden. I've heard them say, "too much work, too little reward." Their plot is grass growing where dirt now stands. They have become afraid of the dark. The part of myself that identifies with the biblical sower whose seed fell on bad ground is also afraid of the dark. Here speaks the child in every gardener, the one who has not been around long enough to know about gardens and gardening and the way unearned failure this year is just last year's unearned version of success. But who is more foolish, the child afraid of the dark or the man afraid of the light? The light will come back in the spring. We will need to have seed in our hand. Our business as gardeners is to outwit the inevitable. The inevitable includes that season that came to Katharine White, as sure it will come to you and me. The best we can hope for is that we get a few things in the ground for someone else's spring. Imagine the grief of those who love and surround us to lose us in the fall and then our color in the spring!

It's not like there are a lot of other choices. People say they don't want to *return to nature* as if there was someplace else! We only have these choices, to plant or not to plant, to grow or not to grow. Gardeners who move to nursing homes have the same choices. They just have to live in the spiritual space that autumn provides all year long. They have to move to the mental memory of the garden and find someone to cultivate that memory.

Here I am not talking about hoeing but about conversation. Maybe the nursing home move, which terrifies everyone who has ever thought of it, needs its own plotting. Perhaps here is the real reason to keep those little garden journals, which I hate so much. They feel so removed from experience. But if one of our moves is to a wheelchair, or we fear it might be, perhaps a journal can be a hoe to our memory, which we'll need in the (gulp) autumn of our years.

These moves all need the same plotting as our garden plot. We don't need reminders of the courage that is needed for gypsy gardening. So many of us use gardening as a hedge against the necessity of moving and changing. We plant a garden so we can look settled. Feel settled. Imagine ourselves as settled down.

The garden I have hoed for two different periods (the nineties and then the year of 2005) was planted and developed by a couple that lived and worked in New York and summered in Amherst, Massachusetts. It remains a superb garden—and I now rent the property, intending to return to it when we retire from New York City. The Browns, the former owners, he of the *New York Times Book Review*, only enjoyed it part of their years. Then, three years after they retired to full-time residency, after, no doubt, desiring that retirement for decades, she died. He managed another three years alone and went to a nursing home in Maine. One year I sent him pictures last year of the herb garden. "Brownie" is now dead. In our backyard in Manhattan we have a sign from his father's chicken farm that we found in the house.

Freedom, someone wise said, is what you do with what has been done to you. Brownie didn't get all that he wanted from his garden. Neither did the one all the neighbors still call Mrs. Brown. When I am in Amherst, I write from her bedroom, overlooking her garden. Amelia Earhart said courage is the price life exacts for granting peace. I need courage to plot the time when someone else will be sitting in what is now *our* place. So did Mrs. Brown. Autumn gardening, the walk-through, the stop, look, and listen at the bedside of the season's dying offering, is the plot for courage.

Once we get this business about necessary moves into our coffin or our cubby in the nursing home, we can begin to fly again. We have the instinct of the rose. I think of our fall behavior as that of the climbing rose. We have to grab on to something and grow toward the light. The real roses do it in the spring; we have to do it in the fall.

There is no reason not to grow a few things in the fall. The entire process is not spiritualized. Turnips and carrots do very well here, under leaves, till early spring. I had three solar tunnels that made fresh spinach a possibility on the Thanksgiving table. At thirty dollars each, they were the best garden investment I have ever made. I had Russian kale that seems to never want to freeze. And the hardy mums last longer every year. But color is what I want. Just a little more to challenge the gray skies of November.

I know I won't get this color, but year in and year out, I search for it. Midge Keeble in her book, *Tottering In My Garden* (1989), tells us "gardening is not the main theme of life. It weaves in and out . . . providing a counterpoint to family, home and friends, giving color and balance to life, challenges unending, and often a dash of the comic."

We can only want what we can't have. We can't always have it. That I want more than I can get from the fall garden is basic. I am working on that theme and counterpoint in my fall desires. Early winter, late fall, whatever we call that time the garden dies, is a great time of the year for embellishing the stage on which the rest of life rests. The *rest* of life needs the spiritual and the physical part of gardening to make it well and interesting. As I see it, we have plenty of time in eternity for the resurrection; now we need time to plot. Remember Frank? He shivered off-season. When it is time to shiver, and be cold and rigid, that is when we should shiver. Between now and then we have plotting to do.

THE AMHERST GARDEN CLUB

THE RITUALS OF LEGACY

THERE IS NO place like the Amherst Garden Club annual May sale.

Octogenarians who have never raised their canes before lift them high over new shades of lantana. The same woman who would have worn a girdle twenty years ago practices deep breathing sliding through the ivies: what if the kind she wants is gone by the time she gets there? Petite grandmothers become petulant over primrose; they wanted the shade that was just sold, and nothing else will do.

The calm that comes from gardening does not prevail in the early morning hours the first few weekdays in May. The gardening sale is the weekend right after the book sale. Right after the League of Women voters removes the dusty smell of old books from the Common, the Garden Club rolls in. Bags with manure sell for a pittance, and they are washed as clean as the garden club's kitchen floors.

The spring in Amherst is a sequence of lawn-ruining events on the town common. The children await the carnival the way the League and the Garden Club await their own spring ritual. With the arrival of the carnival rides on Memorial Day the children finally emerge to ride the rides and spray each other with shaving cream. The smell of lantana and lilac is gone; it has been replaced with that of cotton candy and old grease.

Needless to say, the Garden Club wins the smell contest. At the Garden Club's sale, seven shades of day lilies join signature iris, which accompany the common herbs and lilies of the valley, the white kind that the French call Migues de Bois. I know lilies of the valley constitute a cheap perfume, one that evokes everything I love about the old women who still populate the Amherst Garden Club. They are out of fashion. They are a little strong. They smell of earth and flower.

Would I be accurate in saying that floral variety has decreased as local kitchen floors have become less well scrubbed as women have left home for the workplace? Have briefcases bred brevity in the garden? Is it possible that the subtle scents of modern women belie a certain earlier feminism? I have no scientific data. But I do think we are seeing more of the same and less of the unusual. I am not prejudiced against modern working-out-of-the-home women. I am one of them. But I am prejudiced against zinnias and marigolds and impatiens. True gardeners are allergic to these annuals. We know they are overpriced and under pretty. We believe not only in perennials—like the ladies of the garden clubs—we also believe in rare perennials. We don't want our garden to look like the one next door. Unfortunately too many of my brief-cased sisters live in the suburbs where it is often hard to locate one's own home, so repetitive is the land-scaping. Plus who has time even to weed the marigolds, much less nurture the astilbe?

One year at the Garden Club sale I overheard a long conversation about currants: people remembered the good old days when you could get a bush or two. No one seems to grow them anymore. There are dis-ease issues. I do grow them but only because of my garden inheritance. I inherited in Amherst a perennial garden from one of the masters of the garden club era: she put it in. I just try to keep up with it. She is old school; I am new. At fifty-two, when I was there, I was not young. But when it came to the gardening club ladies, I was just a slip. The ladies (we don't call these people women) LOVED the idea that I had currants. They knew that I didn't know what to do with them, but that's ok. It kept me out of the place where they put women who grow marigolds, and that is what mattered in that moment.

I didn't have the heart to tell the whole story, that I had a dozen mature currant bushes on my property and that last year I failed to pick the currants. The previous year I hired the neighborhood kids to pick them and never got to put them up properly. This past year I took the modern woman's way out: I picked a quart myself, at twilight. I made four jars of magnificent jelly. I used my new berry basket, which ties around my waist with a belt and my new, also store-bought thickener that allows for less sugar and more fruit. I made a complete event out of those four jars and left the rest of the berries on the bush. Small is beautiful. Less is more when it comes to my schedule.

If a member of the Amherst Garden Club finds out, I will be humiliated. What kind of a woman leaves fruit on a bush? What kind of a gardener refuses harvest? The new kind, I fear I will have to admit.

Another year I put an ad in the paper, PICK YOUR OWN CURRANTS. Old German ladies arrived replete with baskets already discolored by fruit. The aprons they wore told me they were serious. As exchange they gave me a jar of their jam. It was more magnificent than mine plus it did not have the sin of waste attached to it. These two picked those bushes clean. I turned myself in to the garden club the next year: They arranged to dig up some of the currant bushes at the right time in advance of next year's sale.

In the old days, at the Garden Club sale, one could get one's purchases signed. The flowers had names, addresses, places from which they came. These were Mrs. Dickinson's euonymus; these were not. These astilbe belonged to Mrs. Smith. They had her signature pink.

(No. Emily Dickinson was not a gardener. Her relatives, however, were. A second cousin is better than no cousin at all.)

I liked naming my purchases for their parents. The peach trees in my garden are called Jean, the raspberries Pat. The yellow day lilies took three years to flower so I renamed them for someone I didn't like as much as the person to whom they actually belonged. Why name plants? Because it assures us that we are better than the garden store, the Walmart's or Home Depot so-called landscaping center. We trade on the real market, made black by the big boxes. In the old days, again, women rarely bought plants. We traded them. Gardening is an underground economy. It is a place beyond the land of money and moneyed time. It now lives suspended between work (currently defined as that which one does for money as opposed to that which produces food or beauty or nurture) and play (a little hobby for the leisured class). Old-time gardening was in a different world; connecting work to food, play to beauty, woman to woman. Money didn't have to come into it at all: we could trade and barter. You cannot imagine how ready plants are to reproduce themselves. The idea of buying a day lily bulb is absurd. They abound underground. They want to be thinned. They beg to be given away—especially since another will return the gift of one. You should see the dahlias I had one year. I didn't pay a cent for them. I did pay some blue and white iris bulbs, if my barter dare be called pay.

Dare we fear for these ladies who battle early on weekday May mornings over the small and the fragile and the plentiful? No. When their breed dies out, and all we have is marigolds and zinnias, then we may begin to fear. If I never see another impatiens spreading uniformly across another suburban "yard," I will be glad. These ladies keep alive the memory of biological diversity and of bartered joy. Their few moments of battle on behalf of the beautiful will be useful for years. These women pick their own currents. They are hardly a dying breed because what they put in the ground will live on and on, way after they are gone. Surely, some of us will be left to divide their legacy and keep it going.

7

THE NEIGHBOR AND THE STOLEN LUPINE

THE RITUAL OF FRIENDSHIP

I MET MY next-door neighbor on the first day I lived in my Amherst house while she was stealing plants from my garden. She was actually "borrowing" perennials from my yard. The previous owner had given her permission to take lupine before we new owners closed on the property. Being a modern herself, she hadn't exactly gotten around to picking up her gift.

Thus, on the first morning in my new house, I met a friend, kneeling at dawn in my garden digging my plants. The sharp steel of her newish shovel glistened in the morning sun.

As I watched her blade touch my earth that earlier day, I didn't know what to say. So what I said is this: I need friends more than I need lupine. We have been friends for years now. I should have mentioned that she is from both a Jewish and Iranian family, married to a man who is Muslim, I am a Christian married to a Jew. We two interfaith families lived side by side for many glorious years. She picked tomatoes whenever she needed from my large plot. I dug in her bank of perennials. One March 30, when it was unseasonably warm, we built a large fire in our back yard (in the duck scale) and let the kids stay up late. Her husband brought homemade cherry wine and got roaring drunk. The kids noticed. Summer nights we watched the kids catch the fireflies in our backyard meadow. We relaxed with each other and forget about the revolution for a while.

One day when Anwar Sadat and Menachem Begin shook a famous handshake on the television, we were both standing there with our boys. My boys were seven and nine, and her boys two and four. The handshake interrupted a basketball game we were all watching. When the two men shook hands, we two both cried. Our four boys gathered round: Mommies, it's only a basketball game. We decided not to tell them the truth and let them think our tears were over the Knicks.

During our friendship, she has fully resupplied my lily of the valley collection and given me some hostas that are the best I know. Lies are told, plants are stolen, even in the gardens and neighborhoods of Eden. Because of friendships like this, I still believe in the possibility of peace, handshakes, non-violent solutions to problems.

Without such friendships, long ago, I would have lived a depressed life alone, filled with flowers and personal property, unviolated. Thank God, she didn't get around to stealing her gift until I had moved in. Now that we have made it through many Bar and Bat Mitzvahs, college graduations, we are on our way to weddings. We once discussed developing the four acres that lie between us. That will have to wait for old age. There are many gardens to borrow between now and then.

8

THE HERETIC IN THE HIBISCUS

THE RITUAL OF REJECTION

WRITTEN TO OFFER explanation and expansion of the *New York Times*, May 2, 2003, article of this title. I tried to join the Garden Club because I knew what I didn't know about Tropical Gardening.

I don't know that I will ever receive a formal letter rejecting me from membership in the Coral Gables Garden Club. I only know because one of my sponsors told me. The reason offered was not my flower arrangements or my bromeliads. Nor is it my lack of enthusiasm about learning tropical gardening. I am a pretty good northern gardener, but the tropics have stumped me more than once. Thus I was prepared to pay the dues, show up monthly, put up with my daughter's ridicule, and get the necessary sponsors. My daughter thought that I was joining the Florida "blue hairs" prematurely. She has insufficient respect for my need for a low-cost personal form of entertainment to get me through my days. Gardening is my hobby—and I have long thought people made too much fun of the folk wisdom of the ladies in the many garden clubs around the world. They know stuff I want to know.

The reason offered to my sponsor for my rejection was that I am "too liberal." I thus join Susan Sarandon in this strange season: she too was uninvited to the Hall of Fame on similar grounds. I join the poets who were uninvited to the White House because they might "embarrass" the president. At least I am in good company.

In hopes to have another chance at membership, I have renamed my French string beans, which are miraculously this March giving a daily crop. From henceforth, they shall be called Liberty Beans. I have also renamed the French lettuces. There is really no need to give the lettuce a nationality. We can just call it lettuce and leave it at that. Similarly, garden clubs could stay out of politics altogether but that is another matter. I have also wrapped my night blooming jasmine in red, white, and blue lights—and put bunting around the orange jasmine. I replanted the gardenia tree in such a way that it could fly a small flag, when the ladies inspect my property, if they feel they need to, when I reapply.

I know inspections aren't always done. Under my circumstances, given that I am not conservative enough for the Coral Gables Garden Club, I thought a little patriotic sprucing up of the yard might help.

The bromeliads could be the problem: the dozens of them in the front yard all spike pink flowers. That may be the origin of the "commie pinko" problem, if that's what it is. Of course, people don't have to go all the way to Joe McCarthy to reject people for membership in the Coral Gables Garden Club. They can think a person is too liberal even if a person doesn't grow an abundance of pink flowers. Plus, the bromeliad garden is simply too splendid to uproot. I will take a stand on the pink flowers. There are some things I won't do—even for membership in the Coral Gables Garden Club.

I am writing a third garden book in order to spruce up my credentials. I was thinking of calling it *Politically Correct Gardening*. Did I mention that when I first came to town the club featured me as a speaker? I used material from my *Spiritual Rock Gardening* book and my *Teaching My Daughter to Mulch* book. They clapped at the end. Many people bought the books. Perhaps they found evidence of my politics in the pages: some of the rocks voted for George McGovern. Some of that mulch voted to remove the Florida Head of Children's and Family Services when she lost someone else's daughter.

In my new book, *Politically Correct Gardening,* I will show the Right way to plant, hoe, seed, compost, and mulch. I will avoid pink flowers all together. Nothing

French will be mentioned. And all plants will wear a compulsory bunting, just in case any member of the Garden Club comes by and wants to salute them.

Wish me luck. I don't know that increased bunting, renaming of plants and flowers, even a new book will give me the credentials I need to become a member of the club. After all, none of these actions addresses the real problem. I am just too liberal.

What's a liberal? A liberal is someone who doesn't take this kind of rejection kneeling on her garden kneepad. She plants it as a seed in your mind. Let it grow.

While I fear the anger growing inside me over my rejection, I also fear the silence that might accompany it, if I stick with courtesy instead of outrage. There are people who would take this kind of treatment sitting down. I have too much respect for seeds so to do: anger seeds grow as well as love seeds in a person's heart.

When I first heard of the rejection, it was four days before Easter, and I had lots of things to do. The Tuesday after Easter, I woke up livid, livid in red, white, and blue, actually. I had laughed when my sponsor first told me. It was a long laugh, one that enlivened my entire office that afternoon. People kept coming in to ask me why I was laughing. I could hardly tell the story, so funny did it seem to me.

I am a little embarrassed at the brouhaha that has resulted from my "leaking" the news to the local press. I called the garden editor of the newspaper, who is a friend, and she took care of getting the story out to way too many people. I never wanted to shame the Coral Gables Garden Club. I never wanted to see them mentioned in the gossip column or to be invited, as a result, to be a member of all the other Miami garden clubs. I also didn't want the city to consider taking away their dollar a year rental at a local hotel— because they discriminate. (I told the city manager that all I wanted was open membership in the garden club, not retribution.) I wanted to join the garden club and participate as a member. I wanted to learn more about tropical gardening from the people who guard the folk wisdom thereof. The seeds I wanted to sow were seeds of color and fun and tropical hope. In order to remove the seed of anger in me, I had to tell my story.

Now I look in the mail for an apology and invitation to reapply. If it doesn't come, I will simply reapply for membership next year. Seeds grow, even under difficult circumstances.

THE RENTED GARDEN

THE RITUALS OF RENTING

I BORROWED A whole garden one summer. My friend was in New York on sabbatical; I was in Minnesota on sabbatical. I was there to learn the language of Social Change. I was a resident of Miami at the time and looking for a good summer spot away from the heat. Many people liken their lives to soap operas; I think of mine as better represented by suitcases, boarding passes, and ground transportation. I am not alone in moving around a lot. Many people do. We also imagine that once motion is our middle name that we can't be gardeners. Gardeners have a lock on the imagery of permanence; people in motion do not. We just need to be more creative to be gardeners.

I had been in New York for a meeting just the week before and had a Broadway meltdown over the smell of lilacs at a Broadway Korean Market. We had moved from Massachusetts to Miami three years ago. I had tried to love Miami summers, but perspiration, rain, and getting to my car before I passed out had become insurmountable obstacles to that affair. In Massachusetts, I loved summer. In Miami, I only loved winter.

The reason for the New York meltdown over the lilacs had to do with both the summer and the bushes I had left behind. (Don't worry, we are going back to Minnesota, by way of Miami and Massachusetts.) I had left behind in Massachusetts three ancient and sturdy lilac bushes: one wine, one white, and one lavender. The smell coming out of the Broadway market evoked a deep loss, not as deep as the loss of the topsoil but deep enough to bring tears to the rim of my eyes. What do Miami and Minnesota gardens have to do with loss and tears and lilacs? They tell us that there are gardens everywhere and that none of them are truly ours. They are all borrowed.

Gardeners falsely imagine that we just can't afford this kind of confusion. We need to be in one place, local not global, local not glocal. Glocal is the increasingly common paradox of having more than one home and more than one garden. Many of us move around all the time and still want the honorific title of gardener to apply to our peripatetic lives.

The day I landed in Minneapolis I put in mesclun in her garden. It came up within thirteen days. I planted by night because I didn't want to miss a second of dirt birthing seed to green. I only had the summer in Minneapolis, and if I didn't plant quickly, I wouldn't see any results.

When I was in New York that spring, having my lilac meltdown, I never could have imagined the gladness of Minnesota. That night in New York, with the lilac meltdown, I bought forty dollars worth of lilacs and took them to my hotel room and figured that would be enough to soothe me. One more broken heart was averted. When I got to my rental in Minneapolis for a month, two lilac bushes overwhelmed me with their scent. Lilacs bloom later out there. I was glad again. Lost pleasure had become found pleasure. I planted flower boxes for my friend, I mowed her lawn. I smelled her flowers for her. I composted for her. Someone was doing the same in my peaked Florida June garden. Somebody is also tending those Massachusetts lilacs even as we speak. We are all tenants on somebody else's earth.

Are any of these plots mine? I don't think so. We rent gardens. We don't own them. I really trembled at digging around in my friend's garden. I had never touched Minnesota soil before. I know the ancient seeds of the prairie are buried there. I even know that their death is the mother of beauty, which is the smartest thing the poet John Keats said. Impermanence causes us to value the moment. What I didn't know till this Minnesota gift of the lilac is about the rent we pay on a garden. Those lilac bushes in Massachusetts weren't even mine. Just another loan from the almighty landlord, who has yet more surprises in dirt for me.

10

THE DAY THEY STOLE
MY COMPOST

THE RITUALS OF DISAPPOINTMENT

HERE IN MIAMI, the semi-tropics, we semi-garden. I do the little stuff, and a horde of men with green taming weapons arrives every other week to do the big stuff. They remove the big dead fronds from the palms, they tackle the bromeliads, they de-fern the ferns. They also steal my compost.

Here in Miami we do global not local gardening. Many of us are transplants and still think that dirt is something already on the ground in which plants grow. In Miami you have to build your own dirt. It does not come with the land.

Every morning I gently carry coffee grounds and cracked eggshells and tomato ends and carrot peels out to my little compost in the back. I add crab grass. I carefully weed from the little vegetable garden I keep, which is both too precious and too small to amount to much, especially since what they call dirt here is actually sand and needs the amendment of compost. You see my circular problem, don't you? It takes a complex sentence to articulate it. In Miami, we have to make our own dirt from other kinds of dirt, carefully arranged and mixed.

Sometimes, if a neighbor with a bad lawn (meaning no chemicals) puts out a pile of grass clippings, I walk the dog over and steal them. I buy the manure in bags: after all, this is a city, and no cow has been seen close by for decades. (Except on New Year's Eve when the populace has imbibed enough to activate its imagination or in East Little Havana where chickens can still be spotted.)

After all this effort to be able to garden, the so-called gardeners come and steal the compost. They take it all. They topple the composter and take the compost. They even rake up under their theft, hoping I will not notice that the compost is gone.

I have tried everything I know to convince "Rubio and Company" that the compost is mine. I have put signs on it, in Spanish, of course. I have left voice-mail messages. I have stood near the composter on the day I know they are coming, Spanish dictionary in hand, trying to write, "No Mierda para Ustedes."

I am not going to post guards. Having a security system in the house is bad enough. I have thought of hiding it so they couldn't find it. And I have considered putting a large cover over it. But these solutions get in the way of aeration, which is important to compost and to me.

I may have to be home whenever they come. The crew changes frequently, and one day on sentry duty at the compost heap does not justice make. Remember: I pay these men seventy dollars per visit to steal my compost! It might be worth a little more to be able to retain it.

Why would I want to stay home and garden, though, on the days that the gardeners come? The other thirteen days per half month are mine; the fourteenth is theirs. Plus, their loud blowers and long machetes would destroy the peace I enjoy in the garden when they are not there.

I could always buy compost in bags, along with the manure. But that would give the gardeners more victory than I intend that they have. Plus, what would I do with my eggshells?

11

THE MANGO AND THE ZUCCHINI

THE RITUALS OF GIFTS

MORE PEOPLE AVOID their friends and neighbors in July than in any other month. In the north, neighbors mean zucchinis. Many people turn out their lights in the evening just to make sure the gardening neighbor next door doesn't stop by with another forty-pound zucchini. He or she is proud of the plant's prowess but has no idea what to do with it at home. It is too good to throw away but not too good to eat, again. These neighbors have already made zucchini cake, zucchini bread, zucchini stir fry, zucchini stir fry flowers, zucchini French fries, zucchini chutney, and zucchini jelly—and still have thirty-nine pounds of zucchini in the refrigerator. This leftover is the last one that turned up in the garden out of a yellow flower, almost from nowhere, in about twenty seconds, when the gardeners weren't looking.

Gardeners take responsibilities for zucchini: we dare not let them rot in the garden without picking them. We waste not and want not. Also, if we don't pick them, next year the "volunteer" seeds—the ones that come up even if you don't plant them, being holdovers from last year—will give us forty forty-pound zucchinis to unload on our neighbors

Here in the tropics, neighbors mean mangos. We would come home and trip over them on our doorstep. We find them on top of our car after a meeting. They show up on our desk at the office. Each proud giver of these awesome gifts tells us that their variety is the best. So far, in my personal contest, not unlike that apple pie eating contest I also ran in the northern fall, the Tommy Atkins is winning. It has a lusciousness that is tart and sweet at the same time. It is soft but not gooey. It resists the black spots on its skin that don't seem to really matter but mess up the fruit bowl's entry into the fruit bowl picture contest.

Surely the word "mango" is just right for the sixty-six-calorie purple/green/red fruit that startles the landscape this time of year. Like tango, mango moves. It gives joy in the speaking. It gives bliss when seen dangling, dangling, abundantly, in colors any designer would choose to entertain sky blue.

The truth, however, must be told. Mangos taste a lot better than zucchinis. Right now they are turning up everywhere: first in the soups, which some people lace with red chilies, to make a near dance out of the meal.

They are showing up in the better salads. Some of us have a husband kind enough to slice one for us each morning, lay it on the counter, and put a grapefruit spoon in it. One boy on Alhambra sets out each afternoon, east of Granada, and sells them three for a dollar fifty. I've even seen kids try to sell coconuts, unopened.

There are many economies, those of the street and those of the grocery store, where they will happily overcharge for a mango. In Coral Gables, the streets and the trash piles are upgrading. We are no longer putting out just any kind of rubbish. We want only upper-end rubbish here—and coconuts are just about right for that. The rest of the stuff we'll have to cart away ourselves or give to our neighbors.

Back to the mango. Some one said that when we choose to work in South Florida, "Half your pay is the bay." I like that notion of salary amendment by things that fall from the sky or float on the water, like the gorgeous views that surround us. One person in a place close to here has actually put out a sign, "Beware of falling coconuts." That sort of liability living really scares me. The alternative is to grace one of our many gates with a more neighborly sign: "Beware of falling mangos." With all these different economies everywhere, I have to remind everyone: I can only meet about three mangoes a day.

12

AN URBAN FARMER
IN MIAMI

THE RITUALS OF UTOPIAN THINKING

(Originally written for the Miami "Prosperity Campaign" of
the Human Services Coalition)

AND THEN I saw the Holy City, the New
Miami.

Wow. A new Miami. What could make
Miami new is liberation from the soft cage of pessimism. This cage is a prison to which we consent and
which we even encourage. It is our cage; we made it
ourselves.

We don't need millions of dollars or millions of
consultants or even millions of ideas: we simply have
to slip out of the soft cage of pessimism about ourselves. The story we tell about ourselves is the problem; it creates its own despair. Were we to tell another
story and imagine another reality, the new could
emerge here with ease.

You know the pessimism: nothing can be done. No
one will do it. We are stuck with poverty, stuck with

traffic, stuck with mean-spiritedness, stuck with a dysfunctional school board, and stuck with crime. Or so we tell each other. We can't afford decent health care. We can't control crime. We can't afford good education. We can't have a good future. We can't be any different than any other American city—indeed, we are winning contests for the worse. We say that we are stuck with this gorgeous sunny city by the sea rather than rejoicing in it. I never sit in a Miami traffic jam without wondering why people put up with such nuisances as delay. I get an answer: the answer is that we think this is the best of all possible worlds. That myth joins pessimism in being a bar on the cage.

The lovely former prime minister of Britain, Margaret Thatcher, coined a phrase for the soft cage of this sulphuric pessimism. "There in no alternative" thus the acronym TINA. TINA is a sure-fire candlesnuffer. How dare you hope for a better world? How dare you? Don't you hear this every day in some way? Nothing can be done, we grew too fast, we grew too funny. The pessimism is the cage. And our imaginations have the key to the cell.

Imagine with me a new Miami, the way the prophets of old imagined a New Jerusalem. To loosen our imagination we might think like urban farmers. Then we wouldn't consider wasting a thing. If any of our children ended up in prison, we would make them work. That's right: make them work. They would make sure there was never a stray wrapper or bottle or beer can anywhere on any of Miami's streets. They would assure that no vacant lot was ugly and instead that it be a park or a garden. When we told the world about who we are, we would say we were a clean city. A city that didn't waste any of its people. Habitat for Humanity would roll its houses into the prisons and once there both build and teach a new generation skills and savvy about life. The idea that I am paying good money to bore useful people burdens my imagination. I know Miami is not the only place to waste human life in jails. I also know that we could supply national leadership by figuring out a way to make use of and educate prisoners and criminals. An old Yiddish proverb says that the heaviest burden is having nothing to carry. It is proven true in the sadness and despair, which haunts our city's prisons and jails.

Prisoners—who are now housed in the equivalent of college dorms, at the same price, without the educational component—would come out of jail to decent jobs through which such jobs the state coffers would be filled. We can't afford to have anyone in Miami, or Florida, or the United States, for that matter who is not a tax-paying citizen. That is waste. When people don't pay taxes, by way of welfare or imprisonment or sheer laziness on their own jobs so that they do not enhance their income, the New Miami alias New Jerusalem is robbed. We can't afford crime. We can't afford to waste prisoners. We can't afford to waste anything on our way to being a world-class, global, and local city. We can't afford workers who work at low wages! Why? Because they don't pay taxes on enough income to matter. Plus, such people are not happy. Imagine telling the world that Miami was a happy, prosperous city, with living wages available for all. Imagine being a city of hope for the prisoner.

To be a place of hope for the prisoners in real jails and the prisoners in the soft cage of pessimism, Miami must create a third and fourth leg to its economy. Otherwise there won't be enough tax-paying citizens to make this place come alive. That leg could clearly be agricultural. The land is here. The garbage to make compost, city wide, is here. The sun is here. The labor is here. Imagine us as the city with the best food, home grown in the world. We would do what ancient peoples have always done well, close the loop and trade with each other. Such an economy is within our reach. In fact, we can start tomorrow by matching restaurant waste to abandoned lots and training people to grow their own food right there. Citywide composting would be next.

Another economic leg that could help us would come from solar energy. Imagine Miami being a place that pioneered solar energy for air-conditioning and other presumed necessities. Imagine being able to brag to the world that business can be done cheaper here.

We already have the world at our glocal doorstep. Miami has such a head start on other American cities by virtue of our location and our diversity. Imagine if we were to take that diversity and location and use it to become a fascinating city, one that wasted nothing and on which nothing was wasted.

We already have a reputation and reality of being a place for fine and exciting art, music, entertainment, and joy. Imagine basing these vibrancies in a real economy, with real money, and a real tax base! If we think we have beauty on our thresholds now, imagine what happens with a little Renaissance energy.

When people say we can't afford the New Jerusalem or new Miami, they are simply not looking at reality. What we can't afford is to waste youth. (The average prisoner is twenty-four.) What we can't afford is to waste soil. What we can't afford is to waste sun. Odd, isn't it, how people think we can't afford to reduce traffic, here in this city where almost nine months a year even seniors could bike if bike paths were built or every other existing road in the grid were simply closed to car traffic. Miami could make the sturdy bicycles as an export after putting them free every five feet all over the city. What we can't afford is the automobile. We can't afford the traffic but mumble non-stop about how there is nothing we can do about it. What kind of people think there is no alternative to traffic?

Imagination cuts through the chicanery of what we can and can't afford. Urban farmers imagine a new Miami, which uses its own resources in such a way as to be marketly and markedly different from the rest of the world. (Some times you have to make up a new world for a new city: "marketly" works because it is about a complete repositioning.)

Once we had an economy, we could have a tax base, which base could provide stunning education and social services, for the few who would still need them. Right now we are a city of great waste, with no educational oomph to change the waste of human lives. This adamantly is NOT the best of all possible worlds.

The best of all possible worlds is to be a healthy, vital, international, energized city, which is different from all the rest by virtue of its economic commitment to end waste and to use people for their own good. (By the way, locally grown food and bicycles could decrease the burden on the health care system also.) Miami has no incentive to be as wasteful and unhealthy as every other American city. We have precisely the opposite set of incentives in our location, our environment, our sunshine, and our people. Why not use what we have to our own advantage?

Why? The answer is the soft cage of pessimism joined by the sorcery of thinking we can't afford options. What we can't afford is to limit our options. The way of life we have right now is much too expensive. Like crime, it wastes rather than renews life.

How do we get out of the cage? We imagine a (really) new city; some might even call it holy. We see, after staring at the alternatives, that utopian alternatives are the ones we can afford. The way we live now is destroying us; it has priced itself out of our market. Real pragmatists see that the common good makes common sense. There are many alternatives, and this is adamantly not the best of all *possible* worlds.

13

THE LADY WITH THE LAWNMOWER

THE RITUAL OF ECONOMY

HER HAIR RESEMBLES her lawn, which resembles her hair—faded, frizzy, simple, and beautiful. She mows the lawn with a push mower about once a week; the job is slow not fast, careful not quick, quiet not loud. She mows circular, doing a small patch at a time. Neither she nor the push mower are getting any younger, thus the dawn suits the task, especially in the summer when even the loud, fast "landscapers" take an afternoon siesta, lying under trees dangerously close to parking spots.

Men in trucks care for most lawns in Coral Gables. They zoom in and zoom out and make a first-class racket. My own "service" rarely remembers to close the gate on the dog run. I guess they're in too much of a hurry. (The dog loves it.)

When I do whole-cost accounting on her way and my way, I see genuine deficit on my side. Neither of us uses chemicals on our lawn (or hair) so there is no comparison there. Our lawns are about the same size. My service involves three men for two hours twice a month, one truck, one mower, three weed whackers, for a total of eighty dollars a month. They do remove death from the trees. They do strew the lawn furniture all over. The service doesn't cost me in time, unless you add finding the dog, replacing the lawn furniture, writing the check, and calling to complain about the gate. But I do pay in the coin of all the fossil fuels, along with the rest of the planet, and the noise does cost me in stress and spirit. Also, I do other work to earn the money to pay the landscapers, and I belong to a gym where I go to get the exercise she gets behind her push mower.

Clearly, she has a bargain, and I do not. It's possible, using this whole-cost accounting that I pay five times what she pays for lawn care. Her clickety-clack approach has advantages my vroom with a view does not. The advantages are exercise, quiet, and cost: in fact she has no cost, save in time directly spent.

Like the Italian Slow Food Movement, she is having idiosyncratic fun. She is preserving a way of life, including her own. I am just getting my grass cut.

When we look at what it costs us to live the lives we live, we are often out of balance. Ozone is really worth much more than $1.89 (then) or $2.46 (now) a gallon and the thirty miles at fifty miles an hour it may or may not get us. Hauling food from places far away, yes, even oranges from Florida, is wonderful, if costly. The truck and its fuel have to be taken into consideration. When I buy compost instead of build it, I do save the five minutes per day it takes to crush the eggshells into the coffee grounds and chop the banana peels up into small pieces. I also forget about having to take the trash out and earning the money that buying my garden soil costs me.

Fast is expensive in a way that slow is not. Efficient is expensive in a way that inefficiency is not. Oddly, most people love to tell us we are "idealistic" when we are really just being cheap. We don't want to pay so much for the services we don't need. We want to save money for what we do need—and for the occasional great food from far away. Those of us who remember the annual orange in the stocking are not so much worried about losing freedom and fossil-fueled abundance of options. What we worry about is being able to afford the good things, like air and water and time and balance.

Right now I pay too much and get too little. She gets her lawn mowed at a bargain while receiving all these benefits. I just get my lawn mowed.

14

REJOICE, THE PAINTED BUNTINGS HAVE RETURNED!

THE RITUAL OF SIGHT

THE OCTOGENARIAN HAD just been told by her doctor that she had very little time left to live. She came to visit about her imminent funeral and to tell me how she wanted it. She also wanted to air a burden, an adult child in deep trouble. Who would take care of her when she was gone?

A few days after the visit, she called with genuine enthusiasm in her voice and said: "The painted buntings have returned!" Her announcement was about the small, colorful birds that migrate to Florida during its spring but the majority of the nation's fall. The message was also more deeply coded. I had chided her during her earlier visit about her silence about herself, her chatter about her daughter. I had tried to suggest it was time to think about herself.

When she told me about the birds and her delight in them, she was letting me know who she is: she is a woman capable of delight in small things. She knows joy despite life-long burden and sorrow. She knows how to see the big in the little.

She was "working" in her garden the day she caught the sight of the returned bunting. By working in her garden, she meant sitting there in the sun watching things grow. One old hippie guide used to say, "If you can't relax, go out, lie down and watch a carrot grow."

I used to take that literally and try to see if I could see a carrot grow. It always beat hoeing. Now I get the joke. There is nothing to see. You just pretend you're watching a carrot grow or working in the garden.

I never leave a workout in my garden without a good look around. In fact, in my favorite garden, the Amherst one, I work an area and ritualize my leave-taking by touching each of the ten plots. I touch them with sight. I stop long enough to see their growth—and how things have changed, usually since just a few days before. Learning to see change is important for both activists and gardeners: otherwise we think nothing is happening when all the while the painted buntings are preparing for their return.

Characteristically, though, even with this great news, my friend began with an apology: "I don't know if I should tell you because you are so busy . . . and you have to sit still for a long time, in the right place, to see the buntings."

I, who talk about myself at the drop of a hat, have few regrets compared to hers. And conceivably less joy as well. I don't always know how to sit still long enough for the return of the buntings. I have missed more than one spring; my friend has not. She knows how to look deeply enough to see. How to see—through the costume of difficulty the world wears—to simple delight, the joy of seasons passing, seasons changing.

Why do we mourn the death of a Palestinian adolescent whose face is blown off by an Israeli soldier? Or vice versa? Because we mourn the springs the boy and the soldier will miss; the returning buntings that they no longer will get to see; the little things stolen from them both by the so-called big things.

Why do we get chills at a car crash, mourn a thirty-seven-unit low-income apartment building wiped out in a nameless flood? Because we don't see the strangers who did stop as we passed by, the manager who took in the dog of one of the residents. He didn't have to take in her dog. He could have stayed aloof—and missed the buntings, ignored the spring, been defeated by the mountain of trouble that the little birds fly over and seed with joy.

As some people miss every train they should have caught, most of the life they should have lived, other people pause. Other people pay attention. Other people notice that they are alive and are glad. Other people "work" in gardens so as to find a way to see.

Sometimes the people who notice the most are the people with the most distraction, not just the modern, well-credentialed distraction of being "so busy," but the universal credential of dolor, suffering, genuine first-class trouble.

People with brain tumors stop by the church and talk about how they are going to manage to wait for the next MRI. I press them: How will you manage? "Fly fishing," they announce.

Old men who live alone send greeting cards from the World War II Memorial—and fly through deep scars by telling a story or two from the world the greeting card remembers for them. Little stories challenge big wars.

Scripture announces: "Weeping may Endure for a Night but joy cometh in the morning" (Psalm 30:5). My caller was telling me the same thing. She was talking about her death, her life, her birds, and her spring. She had no reason to have so much confidence in her next season. In her announcement, she was telling me her name. Her name is irrational hope. She was telling me that she was going to die the way she had lived.

As every third word we hear on the news is deficit, it may be time to notice the opposite. The asset. The assets. If people on the edge of the grave can notice the return of the buntings, so can those of us a few feet away. They will be the ones to remind us that the garden will take care of those we can't when we can't take care of them any longer.

15

INTERMEZZO—
THINK OF THIS CHAPTER
AS THE SHERBET COURSE

THE RITUAL OF LETTING GO

I LEFT MIAMI with a broken heart. I loved my church but my partner, Warren, could not get a job there as a tenured history professor. He was willing to continue his weekly commute from Hartford to Miami and back. I couldn't accept the gift. It was too expensive.

I salved my wound with the Amherst garden. We hadn't sold the house and instead had rented it to tenants who were rapidly destroying the perennial gardens. We could go "back" to it. I had hired a magnificent person to consolidate and save what she could with my long-distance absurd supervision. She took control of things and moved the far gardens closer to the house and actually turned the old kitchen garden into a splendid perennial forest. I was thus able to carry my broken heart north with a little hope off to the side: I could now garden again with vigor in the right kinds of season with the right kinds of soil. I could return to a garden club that welcomed me. I made enormous plans—and also remodeled most of the house. Domesticity was mine for the year that we were back in Amherst. Our more settled friends were very kind and accepted us without question. They even helped make the garden beautiful again. But more than one dinner party included wisecracks such as, "First you leave Amherst for Chicago, then you leave Amherst for Miami, I wonder where you will leave Amherst for this time." Ah.

We left Amherst for New York on Christmas Day, 2006. I talked the "alternative" movers into shrink-wrapping the Christmas tree with the ornaments on it. We moved it into Stuyvesant where it did not stand up straight but certainly gave new meaning to the words "gypsy gardener."

16

CARRYING COMPOST
TO UNION SQUARE

THE RITUAL OF USELESSNESS

WHY DO I bother on Mondays, Wednesdays, and Fridays, sometimes Saturdays to carry a little bag of coffee grounds, eggshells, lettuce leaves, and the occasionally interesting vegetable butt to Union Square? I live on East Eighteenth Street, I work at Washington Square. It is on my way. I put the compost wannabe in a plastic bag and carry it the three blocks west and two blocks south while also carrying my backpack and usually some other oddball so-called necessity. I bear my burdens judiciously, trying very hard not to overload my arms and back. I keep one hand free for the compost and load up the other with the preposterous item of the day. If we've had a party and there is lots of compost (never meat leavings), I get someone to carry the other bags.

When I get to the Union Square Greenmarket, the

bucket is there admonishing care for the earth and showing outcomes. There are demonstrated three gradations of soil: good, better, and best. My garbage becomes her dirt. The woman who staffs the compost site is usually cheerful and clearly has other customers. Most people take food away from the market, others and I bring it. We carry in; others carry out. Without us, the others couldn't carry out. With us, the soil has soul.

I know there are very few of us—nine bags at most when I get there about 10 a.m.

We can hardly call this a movement in a city of millions of people eating food, drinking coffee, and cracking eggs. I also know how many bags there are in the late afternoon because once I managed to slip my American Express Card and some money into one of the bags. My son and husband had to go looking for it as I was "uptown." Anyway, the man who went through the compost for us got a nice tip and my card is now composting somewhere upstate with about ten singles wrapped around it. Now you see just how committed I am to composting!

I know I could put my leftovers into my garbage and that the city would tote them off. My doorman would even take the garbage cans out. All I would have to do is take the garbage to the can. I don't need the extra miles.

I also know that my petite, nearly flimsy, daily coffee and eggshell hardly a garden make. I even know that compost takes a year to make—and that my widow's mite of an offering hardly creates enough dirt for a proper beet to grow in.

Additional reluctance to carry comes from getting my work clothes dirty, the rare smell, the water I use in getting clean after I bag the would-be dirt.

The number of reasons not to compost includes the frequent rain, cold, and general irritability that comes with adding burden to the burden of being an on-foot New Yorker. Tote bags abound—and it is a daily matter to keep them light. Many of us play great games around this issue. Keeping more than one pair of shoes at the office, never taking work home (ha), reading slim as opposed to fat books. Not carrying a lot of change. All these little matters compete with the compost-carrying adventure. Seriously, why bother?

The only reason I have for bothering is that it is a ritual for me. It is a soil-reminding ritual. It is a way for me to do the earth-to-earth and ashes-to-ashes and dust-to-dust thing on a regular basis, just so it doesn't surprise me later in life. It is also a way to be reminded of my earthiness, my great reliance on the confluence of a little dirt and a little water, without which I would cease to exist. It is also an act of miracle mimicking: how does that stuff go from white shell to black dirt, green leaf to light soil? I like the idea of being a little part of a miracle on a regular basis.

I also like the idea of reverence for the earth that moves under my feet. I am enchanted by food: Why not be enchanted by the process of making food? How do we make food? Not by opening the package. We make food by growing it. How do we grow it when we live on East Eighteenth Street??? We grow it by participating in nature's miracles. We throw our contribution into the soup pot. We eat what we grow.

Rather than being estranged from dirt, my composting escapade allows me to befriend dirt. This friendship even helps me with my radical's self-righteousness problem, a perennial if there ever was one. I think I am so clean, so correct, so Goddamn right about everything. Global warming: they should have asked me first. The War in Iraq: I told them. That is why I am enjoying the government's failure so much. It proves how right I was. I don't even get to the body bags, the amputees, and the fact that the money we are spending will impact my grandchildren's entire future. I stick on the clean green I told you so—and from there spit. Spitting is not a good game for a radical. We need strategies, not spit.

So my ritual helps me to get dirty. Getting dirty is so much better for me than getting clean: it keeps me composted. It keeps me hopeful that my soil can yet become soul.

That's why I carry my compost to Union Square: so that my soil can yet become soul and my soul, soil.

17

PIGWEED

The Ritual of Surprise

As I said in the Intermezzo, I had to leave my garden in Amherst and move to New York. The job was too good not to go. So I left my perennials and my big vegetable patch and richly prepared soil and settled on a monthly trip back to the country. My first trip back gave me a gardener's surprise: the vegetable patch had been taken over by the good weeds. Daisies had inched out the sticky green stuff, the pigweed, the ugly version of amaranth. A flowing sheet of white replaced green oddball chaos. How did the garden manage to look better than it ever had when I weeded it every day? How did those daisies beat that perennial powerful pigweed? Similar things had happened in the day lily patch: they had spread and were the master of the mint. The opposite had been true the previous year: the mint had moved into the lawn, not just the daylilies.

The garden is often a site for miracles. Curses turn to blessing; even those long-seeded curses can turn to blessings. We may or may not be the architects of those blessings. They may just "Happen." Hector Aristizabal, a Columbian exile, left his country after being tortured there. For the last twenty years Aristizabal has run "The Theatre of the Oppressed" in California. There he works with ex-offenders, gang members, at-risk youth, kids who are on the street because they have nowhere else to go. He works with them around initiation rituals —which he argues are often forms of self-torture. We scar ourselves, we do something that scares us to death, and many young women cut themselves today. Hazing practices are often like torture, locking people up and the like. Why? Kids say they cut themselves to stop the hurt. Aristizabal says that the United States is a culture of death because its rituals around death are so paltry. Think of the way we die, tubed, wearing a hospital uniform, in a sterile room, he says. He argues for a new way of death and a new way of life. He no longer tortures others because he was tortured. He is a curse turned to blessing kind of guy. Like a garden, not a gardener, but a garden, he performs miracles. He turns the way of the weed into the way of the flower.

My daughter, Katie, and I were in jail protesting Guantanamo detentions and tortures three days before the Supreme Court ruled against it. One of the women in our jail cell was a woman named Frances Crowe. Frances is from Northampton, where I used to live. She came down for the action. She is eighty-seven years old and was head of the American Friends Service Committee for many years in Western Massachusetts. The last time we were arrested together I was nine and a half months pregnant with my now twenty-three-year-old son. Frances must have been sixty-four. We were arrested for sitting in at Silvio Conte's office in Holyoke against U.S. intrusions in El Salvador. Conte changed his vote soon after that—and it had nothing much to do with our little protest. We were part of the 100 blows against the tree, each of which cuts it down, not just the last one.

The cops that day just couldn't see their way to arrest a blown up, overly pregnant woman, an old lady, and the nun that joined us. Frances remembered the story, as did I, as we sat in at the 7th precinct. We find our tough dove identity in that ritual, the ritual of non-violent direct action, the stories we get to tell about it. The songs we sing, this last time Christmas, Broadway, Peace and Justice as the encore. Frances tells of a new ritual she has learned now in many jailing with older women. Think Granny Brigade. When it looked like we had run out of songs, and still had time to go, Frances suggested a new ritual. She said that the nine of us could each do a personal consult on our health. We could each have fifteen minutes of talking about our personal aches and pains and get advice from each other about what to do. She said she has done this the last couple of times she has been incarcerated and that it was just wonderful. She was disappointed when we got out a few minutes after thinking about this ritual. She wanted the consult.

Frances was trying to turn the little curse of our little day in jail into a little blessing. I garden because gardening is the fight with the weeds on behalf of the flowers. Absurdly little, isn't it? Gardening, I mean. Even when we ignore the garden, the pigweed can sometimes be defeated by its own meanness. Daisies thrive by effort and its absence. Rituals, conversations about ache and pains are often as good as a visit to the Mayo Clinic. Little dramas at the United Nations will finally stop the torture. Larger things turn us into the very totalitarians we oppose. Dumb luck will have to do for the daisies. Small things will surprise us in overturning torture. But the rest of the garden plots (there are eleven left even after the while we were in Miami Consolidation) deserve a little more reflection. Just because effort and sizable power are not always necessary for the transformation of curse to blessing doesn't mean they aren't useful. Sometimes we have to pull the weeds out. Sometimes we have to weed until we hurt. Other times we can play tricks with weeds. Once I decided to name some particularly different weeds flowers. Unlike the pigweed I just couldn't fight them anymore. They had won. I named some of the uglier weeds, the purple flowery things that hurt your arm when you pick them, into flowers. I stopped pulling them out and let them have the raspberry patch. Reframing weeds into flowers is as good as living here all the time. Training my eye to see the blossoms in the flower patch also helped: I no longer have the time to weed so instead of the gardener's perfectionism I so long enjoyed and tormented myself with is gone. I see the flowers, I ignore the weeds. These tricks of the mind are sometimes all I have to offer. Gardeners never have enough time; now I have even less in Amherst. The pigweed could beat me in the long run. But not if the daisies self seed.

PART TWO

GARDENING BEYOND PLACE

18

GLEANING

THE RITUAL OF FRAGILITY

THERE IS A famous painting by the nineteenth-century French painter, Jean-Frances Millet, in which two women stand in a field, "gleaning." The poor were allowed in to pick up what the rich didn't take. They paid attention to what was left behind. I want my gardening to do the same: to pick the fields clean and to prohibit waste. I think of it as a new version of dumpster diving, a habit I join the poor in having. Ritualizing an attention to what otherwise might be wasted is an important ritual for an activist. We don't want *anybody or anyhing* left behind.

Churches on the eastern end of Long Island stock their soup kitchens by picking up the potatoes left behind by the picking machines for their soup kitchens. A man died in New York City having worked the streets every day of his life. He left behind

a garage full of working toasters, heaters, blenders—
all of which had been thrown out by a fellow citizen.
He had sold enough to bequeath over a million dollars to the city. He lived the life of a scavenger. I think
too of Farm Share in Homestead, Florida, which
receives and delivers nationally tons of vegetables "too
ugly" to ship. Started by one woman going through a
difficult divorce, at the suggestion of a grower who
wanted to get rid of the high fees he was paying in
garbage pick-ups, Farm Share now supplies soup
kitchens around the country. Imagine the pressure on
a tomato or a squash: it must look perfect to go to
market, just like many of us must look better than we
do in order to go to market ourselves.

Similar underground commercial practices exist as
well. I think of the joy of a yard sale or of thrift shops
and the way they costume beyond the market-niched
boutique that displays only one kind of clothes for one
kind of person. In a thrift shop, everyone gathers to
recycle their wares and to recycle their costumed iden-
tities as well. Today I can be a businesswoman, tomorrow an aging hippie. I haven't been "typed," that
wonderfully frugal version of the word "stereotyped,"
on the way in. I don't have to wiggle out of a box that
marketers have made for me. I can wiggle into a short
skirt in the back of the shop when no one is looking.
Of course, that's not "me," but then again where else
might I have the freedom just to see if it might be?
The joy of a yard sale is the same: we may find almost

anything. The Chelsea Flea Market on any given Saturday morning is a shopper's paradise, especially a shopper who doesn't want the ugliness of box stores or the conformity of the boutiques. There you can shop out of the box. The hunt is as interesting as what happens. We not only save an object from the dust of someone's garage; we also keep it out of the landfill.

GLEANING IS AN environmental practice of some significance. It reduces waste while intensifying pleasure. It magnifies objects because they get to have a second and third life. Some things are just too good to throw away. That's why they end up at the "white elephant" gift giving of groups at Christmas or at church rummage sales or in yard sales. They are being recycled, and the practice is not only economic and environmental. It is also spiritual. It says we care. Recycling spent on unwanted goods says we care about not filling the earth up with junk and that we care about filling up others with tortured vegetables and "too good to toss" clothing.

What is spiritual about gleaning is that it carries care. It pays attention to the edges and the corners, the garbage heaps and the tossed away. It says out loud that vegetables don't have to be perfect to be allowed out in society.

Gleaning is an attitude as well as an act. We shop the yard sales. We save the ugly vegetables. And we also liberate: we take things out of closets and let others have at them. When we clean our cellar, we do the same thing. We rescue and liberate from the dustbin. Trash becomes treasure. If attics contain our past, then so be it. Everything, to the gleaner, does not have to have an immediate use. We can rotate uses.

Spiritually, the ugly and almost used up, the snarled squash and the bruised tomato, are the stuff that too many of us are made of. I think of all the people either on disability or hoping to get disability. Something broke in them. They fell off a roof or a ladder. They had a car accident. They got hurt in a crime. Now they are no longer perfect and can't be sent to market. Gleaners still care about people like this: we go to the field and save them.

Gleaners love Habitat for Humanity's jail project. It trains prisoners to build houses. A flat-bed truck wheels the house into the jail where time and life is being wasted. And it teaches electricity as well as building a house. When the house is done, the truck takes the house to its location. Gleaners find use for people whom others think are useless. Gleaners hate to see time or people wasted. Likewise, gleaners treasure what isn't done at the end of the day as much as what is. We relieve ourselves of the anxiety of the to-do list. We treasure what remains in the field as much as we like what is picked and used and perfectly so. I decorate my garden with broken shards of my favorite dishes. They become places to hold the hose when I water. And they help the seasons along. Even in seasons without color, I have color in my garden. And I don't have to say good-bye to my broken pieces. They remain with me, holding the hose and the memory of when they graced my table.

I once made a Christmas garden, which was an Easter garden, too. We had fifty-five poinsettias left over from the Christmas service. No one wanted to take them home as they had dried out and were drooping. In South Florida we had almost no dirt, only sand and coral rock. I was always composting, buying dirt and fertilizer just to grow a few gnarled tomatoes. I took all the poinsettias home, turned them on their bottoms and watched my new garden appear every day. I added the Easter lilies too. And I took all the pots back to the garden store. They were very happy to have them rather than to see them end up in the you-know-where. These plants had a good life while blooming; they may as well have a good life as dirt. Most of us hope for the same for our bodies. When they say ashes-to-ashes and dust-to-dust over us, we hope our bottoms will turn up good soil. When I think of resurrection, I will be able to think of this soil I built, gleaned from the old flowers.

Gleaners also save seeds. We hang on to things that others let go by. How else would we have forty-five varieties of apples or heirloom tomatoes, if someone hadn't bothered with the inefficiency of saving seed? "The best time to plant a tree is yesterday" according to the Native Americans. Why would anyone waste a seed that could be gleaned for its future glory? That is another thing gleaning does. It gleans future glory. It sees in the past a future. It sees in the old something new. It sees in the useless something useful.

Gleaning satisfies that urgency in us for something new and shiny. Yes, we have that urgency. Even those of us who are the most radical of environmentalists know it. We want things around us; we treasure objects. Gleaners find great stuff in other people's garbage. We walk the streets in the better neighborhoods early on trash day just to make sure no good things are going the wrong way.

Gleaners save stuff. We are deeper than recyclers. We take what others can't use and make use of it. We are scavengers of the sacred and enjoy the surprise of finding what we didn't know we needed. Like my favorite bookstore in the hills of western Massachusetts, we "sell books you don't need in a place you can't find." And that's the fun of it, the finding, and the seeing what is left behind.

Gleaners are actually more selfish than compassionate. Sure, we can give away some of what we glean, but why would we? Mostly gleaning is a consumer's adventure, a low-cost form of personal entertainment, a way to be a "shop till you drop" type without spending any money.

As selfish and personal as it is, gleaning also has great capacity to give to others. It is the utmost in both health and environmentalism. Feeding people is about as close to health as you can get! And yet we don't do a very good job of feeding people, even those of us who have the money to buy food. Too much of it is so heavily packaged that we can't even get to it. Then there is the subject of the poor themselves. They are the thrown away.

In the old days we went to worship carrying a canned food to "feed the poor." People with something in their cupboard brought something for those without anything in their cupboard—and a charitable exchange occurred. We increased these efforts around the holidays, which always bothered me. Weren't people hungry in February as well as November?

With or without my approval of the method, these canned goods "drives" flourished. The congregation got the food to the poor—either by a direct hand out at the parish gate or by a food bank open a few days a week. In the most recent generation of hunger action, we send all the food to a central location, which not only gathers donations but also buys in bulk.

There is an even newer generation in hunger action—and it couldn't come a minute too soon. This iteration is based in a very smart thought, which I first heard stated by Duco Hamasaki, warrior of Miami's state-of-the-art Daily Bread Food Bank. "It takes more than food to stop hunger," he said. Now that got my gleaner's attention. Gleaners use what we can find and we use it well—and canned goods just don't make enough sense as a way to care for the poor.

Canned goods are a good ritual—and what we need are more systemic rituals.

The Daily Bread Food Bank is a state-of-the-art assault on hunger because it buys and distributes and stores—in a serious warehouse—what people need. It uses what Farm Share finds. It also uses peanut butter and tuna fish, not cranberries, cranberries, cranberries. Why do I diminish the cranberry? Because I have seen parish food banks fill up with them annually for almost thirty years in the ministry.

This cranberry bit is not gleaning: it is getting rid of what we don't want. Gleaning finds and uses or gives away what we do want! I recall the time we had a "cranberry scare" in Massachusetts: that year these potentially flawed products flooded the food banks. It was not a pretty sight. In the name of spiritual generosity, something much sneakier was happening. This action reminded me of nothing so much as a woman on my bus on a tour through China. Every time we stopped, the hungry children would swarm the bus. She would donate a penny to each, as soon as she gave her camera to someone who could snap her generosity.

Poverty and hunger are smart. They have managed not only to survive but also to increase. Even the best of gleaners are still going to bed hungry, in every city and town in America. On that ground alone, caring people evaluate their action against hunger. We have long found our canned food drives wanting. We feared they might have been more we did for our own Holiday spirits than for the tables of others.

Picture the Homeless in New York City is a similar project. How do we care for the homeless? We attack housing policy and make developers build low-income and middle-income apartments every time they put up a high rise. We paint orange the abandoned houses and yell out loud that people need homes not shelters.

Gleaners live the high life in a low-cost way. We save. We care. We can. We keep our eye on what is left behind and from there live healthy, earth-caring lives.

19

SACRED CHOW

THE RITUAL OF EATING

GARDENING IS ONE of the least efficient occupations of all time. I figure every tomato I ever grew is worth about twenty dollars. My appreciation of how much time and effort, land use and seed cost slowly combine to create a beautiful fruit is the reason I am so fond of the Slow Food Movement. I know how sacred chow is. I know what slow means to food.

I also know what fast means to food, which is to say crunchy, salty, blobs of congealed fat, which one eats quickly in order to not have to face the question of whether it is chicken or fish, hamburger or dog food.

Fast has other problems beyond its nutritional and taste poverty: it comes in paper and from ugly buildings. It reinforces a value called "fast" and people who are as efficient as I am don't like fast. We like efficient.

There is a difference. Fast fries out the quality in food; slow fries it in.

Think of a good stew. On the first day, the vegetables and the meat have not learned how to make love. They are fumbling around under the covers. The following days, they are intimately connected and each bite contains the other. The seasonings have married.

The matter of whose labor is involved in the stew and the tomato and the so-called whopper is also of import. Kids get jobs in fast-food joints and even speak themselves of how small and little they are when they get those jobs. "I ain't ever going to get out of this McDonald's." Ouch. People who grow food as good as a tomato and know how to make a good stew are people who feel good about themselves. They are not cursed; they are blessed.

Now there is FINALLY a movement called the Slow Food Movement. Both Terra Madre and Salone de Gusto are events organized by the Slow Food Movement. Terra Madre is the meeting of world food communities that happens in Turin, Italy, in October, and the Salone de Gusto is the most gentrified of gourmet food producers gathered anywhere. It makes Dean and DeLuca look downscale.

Terra Madre is a project of Slow Food, coordinated in the United States by AG Innovations Network. Five thousand producer participants came to the second one, which is the only one I have been able to attend. I wanted to go to the third this year but my son got involved in a national championship and I had to turn in my ticket. I adore his championships —but also couldn't believe I was eating Sarasota, Florida, food all weekend instead of tasting the world.

At Terra Madre, the word "whopper" was mercifully removed from our ears. There were six official languages: English, Italian, Spanish, French, German, and Russian. Two thousand producers came from western Europe; 500 from those nations formally known as the Eastern Block; 400 from Africa; 500 from Australia; and 1300 from North and South America.

Prince Charles closed the conference by quoting Ruskin, "Industry without art is brutality." Everyone there knew what he meant. Las Semillas, the seed savers, from Mexico had organized a cooperative meeting during the entire conference to organize coffee producers in fair-trade approaches. Carlo Petrini, the movement's charismatic founder, also spoke and said he never wants to see the label "Slow Food" on anything mass-produced. In response to anyone who wondered at his extraordinary ability to line up corporate sponsorship for rural and defiantly uncommercial traditions he said, "I haven't sold my soul yet, and at my age it's too late anyway."

Carlo Petrini defines the Slow Food Movement as "an eco-gastronomic movement. We were born as a gastronomical association, paying attention to the traditional pleasures of the table and wine, in order to oppose in some way the crazy speed of the 'fast life'—the way of life and food production that leads to the homogenization of flavor and the erosion of culture."

Whenever I say to people that I am interested in the Slow Food Movement, they roll their eyes. They imagine me as a second generation of hippie or crunchie or foodie—all of which is part of the truth. The larger truth though is that I like to eat. I like to eat raspberries that taste like raspberries and tomatoes that taste like tomatoes. I see no point in living in a world where you can get a bad tomato twenty-four hours a day. I like things that make living living—as opposed to something we do for the convenience of survival or corporations. As a gardener, I am happiest when I have dirt under my fingernails. I feel connected to what matters. Spiritually, I know I depend on a little water, a little seed, and a little sun to live. Without these ordinary miracles (forget the big stuff), I don't live. I don't eat. Indeed we all eat to live but many of us also live to eat. We like the feast, the grand buffet of life. Without good food, we aren't happy.

Food is sacred chow. It has the function of keeping us biologically alive—and spiritually alive. So often we forget the sources of our food. We turn food into a sacred cow—a thing that we use and use up and do so unconsciously. We insult biodiversity. We insult earth, air, water. We act as if farmers aren't behind cellophane packages of beef or peas. They are! There is great tension between sacred chow and the sacred cows that attach to food and its production and its eating in our society. The Slow Food Movement rebalances this tension and links farmer again to food.

By slow food I do not mean precious, gourmet food, sold by celebrity chefs and prepared according to recipes in glossy cookbooks. I mean food that is authentic, that has been grown and prepared using methods that are local, organic, and sustainable. Eat sometime in the diner in Newport, Oregon, called Local Ocean. In that restaurant there are not only a dozen kinds of fish, they also report how each was caught and where it was caught. By local food I mean food that is as simple and tasty as a hamburger, without the polluted, agribusiness origins of the fast food restaurant versions. I mean something that is efficiently grown and understands that quality takes time. I mean whole-cost accounting, a term Hazel Henderson popularized as an economic measure. Enough hamburgers, and especially their trans fats, can kill you. Why would a three-dollar meal on a regular basis be worth years off your life?

How can you or I live a slow food life?

    a. Start with salads. Grow them. Rotate the greens in a very small plot and or container. Work up to a full garden . . . but don't think you need to garden big to garden. If you don't have land, join a community garden.

b. Cook on weekends and rotate what you have frozen by month. Work the secondhand shelves at the local markets. Make stew of the vegetables and eat them a day after you have cooked them.

c. Learn the art of the international picnic. Carry your own utensils and containers (get rid of Styrofoam takeouts). Buy beautiful containers and keep a tablecloth in your lunch bag.

d. Learn to cook for a crowd and organize a convivium, the local unit of the Slow Food Movement.

e. Become the person who perpetually brings the best dish to the potluck. Compete with yourself and others. Make the store-bought coleslaw and potato salad look bad. Turn both items into socially disapproved fastness.

f. Refuse to eat on the run. Take a real lunch hour.

g. Join the Local Slow Food Movement, Communities Involved in Sustainable Agriculture (CISA), make a contribution and get involved.

h. Join a Community Supported Agriculture Project, with a friend splitting your share or not. The Western Massachusetts Food Bank is one of several. By joining you help not only the hungry but also yourself. In New York for $400.00 a year we get vegetables from upstate farmers that are fantastic. Yes, we have to haul the stuff. It tastes thrice as good as anything even at the Farmer's Market—and costs a lot less.

i. Make Compost, build soil as a way of life. Make a ritual out of your eggshells and coffee grounds. You will not be disappointed.

j. Learn to use the word Glocal. You live locally and globally.

Chow is sacred. Nothing but a little time and a little self-respect is in the way of any of us eating and enjoying sacred chow.

20

GETTING REAL ABOUT FOOD

THE RITUAL OF FOOD REALITY

IT WAS EARLY evening, I was really hungry and the only relief in sight was the Ramapo Thruway so-called service station. I put gas in the car and went in to see what gas they had for me. I grew up before the thruway went in and listened to nothing but my extended family's extended conversations about how the road would destroy upstate. Later in my life, as the contracts were let for which agribusiness would manage the food on the thruway, I wrote an article about local food. At the time I didn't know what the local food movement was, just that local restaurants, instead of franchises up and down the automotive spine of the state, might be a way to limit the damage. I proposed to the Thruway Commission that local owners put up locally owned restaurants at each exit. That would make driving more interesting and keep fast food from threatening the feast of life. I imagine pork and sauerkraut at Exit 19, arugula salad at exit 20, etc. I was confirmed last Wednesday night as I sought nourishment in Ramapo.

Anyway, searching for my meat in due season, I realized there are only two franchises at Ramapo. One is McDonald's and the other is Uno's, a pizza place. I settled on the pizza place only to observe that the warming tray was dead empty. I practically wept as I asked the young woman behind the counter if there was any hope for one such as I to get a pizza. "Sure, she said, "I'll make it fresh for you." "You will! How long will that take?" My thoughts went utopian, and my stomach gurgled. I was both thrilled at the idea of slow food on the thruway and distraught at waiting for a freshly made pizza. She took care of my gurgle and left my utopia alone. "One and a half minutes," she said. So it was that I entered my own country of ambivalence about food. I want it slow and I want it fast. I want it local and I want it cheap. Mostly, when it comes to food, I want it now. When we have it now, it tends to taste like that "Fresh" pizza in Ramapo. Its virtue was that it was warm. Its sin was that it was made of something that long ago was grain, the white flour, and something long ago, the tomato, that was fruit. The cheese was no longer cheese, and if the pepperoni ever was food, I'll be surprised. As I wolfed down my warm glob of chemicals, I thought about the sources of my food. In Florida the tomato pickers get a pittance a

bushel. Nobody could possibly pay the migrant workers any more than that because otherwise I'd never get
that round warm 800-calorie, nutritionally worthless
globule for just $6.99. You have to add the truck and
its gas, the middleman's middleman's middleman, the
lawyers they hire to fight the migrants so they don't get
more for picking the tomatoes.

Then there are advertising costs to make me want
the pizza. The union-busting lawyers who make sure
the woman who made it fresh for me doesn't make
too much money. Then there is the package, which is
at least 11 percent of the product. They don't charge
me for eating this stuff in the car while driving down
the thruway. That pleasure is free. The culture of fast
food is amazingly conformist, boring, tasteless and
unhealthy—and people think that the Slow Food
Movement is a "weird" idea. You figure.

I remember my church in Miami with more fond-
ness than is probably legitimate. That doesn't mean I
like everything about it. Because some New England
Yankees founded the congregation in 1925, every year
on the Sunday before Thanksgiving, there used to be a
pilgrim festival. The whole congregation had pilgrim
outfits and pilgrim hats. The women would sit on one
side of the congregation and the men on the other, just
like in the days of yore, 1,200 miles north. The minister would read long-winded proclamations. Tableaux
of live pilgrims would be the backdrop on the altar.
Someone carried a big musket he had brought down

from Boston. He led the procession with his wife who carried an old Bible in with the gun.

Someone, not me, suggested the second year I was there that we might do a different Thanksgiving celebration. I foolishly and wisely agreed. We might have people from every nation that had migrated to Miami stand and wear some form of native dress and read some work from their own culture. The first year we had eleven nationalities in tableaux—one Pilgrim, one Peruvian, one Yankee, a Cuban, a Mayan, a Russian, a Dominican, a Parisian, a Haitian, a Nicaraguan, and a Mexican. It was incredibly beautiful and moving— and made its point about who we were as a congregation. One of the sweetest older ladies in the congregation came up to me afterward, "Please, please, please, don't tell me we have to eat their food, too. It just won't be right." What we eat is full of cultural prohibitions and permissions. What we eat is either a Eucharistic feast or a human folly. What we eat is emotional. What we eat is who we are. When we eat bad food in cars on thruways, that is who we are.

In the long series of conversations that followed this retabling of the tableaux, the word "right" was used way too often. "Right" is just another way of saying purity code. Who is to say who eats right? When we say, "I hope we don't have to eat their food, too" what we are saying is that we hope feast never comes. We hope Eucharist never comes. We hope against justice at table and for the right ways of doing things.

What is feast eating? It is the following out of Genesis 2:15, the Lord God took the human into the garden and told them to till it and keep it. One garden, one humanity, one table coming from one garden. Back to the garden is feast eating. Real eating is supposed to be feast eating with everyone at the table of origin. We are to retable the tableaux.

But something very strange has happened to food in the richest country of the world. We can get a bad tomato just about any time of day in any season. We eat out of paper bags and drink the magnificent beverage of coffee out of Styrofoam cups. While we are drinking the coffee, we worry about the possibility of nuclear war over oil. We eat alone. We eat while driving. We eat, but there is nothing sacred or beautiful or slow about it. My own people come to meetings and leave half a foreign country's worth of paper and Styrofoam behind. We have our coffee hour with paper cups. Kids eat chicken fingers over and over again—and slow food has to organize as (an increasingly popular and fast growing) international movement. Imagine having to organize politically for the right to eat slowly and well. The fast food economy has created a world in which we have to protect ourselves from it.

Fast is the enemy of feast. In this post-modern, supposedly wonderful world, many of us no longer know how to eat, or sleep with the peace of a shepherd. Imagine giving up eating and sleeping in order to follow orders about how to eat and sleep. Remember, she falsely said, "I can make that for you *fresh*." When we get *real* about food, we look like utopians to others. They make fun of us as silly and wide-eyed. One look at her pizza and one made fresh ought to take that argument straight to the landfill. Every interaction in good food is slow, whole, just; every interaction in fast food is fast, distorted, tasteless and unjust. Who is the utopian? And who the fool?

21

THREE WOMEN AND THE THEOLOGY OF THE GYPSY

THE RITUAL OF THINKING

THE GARDEN HAS always been a seriously spiritual place. As such it has needed a theology, a picture of its God. There have been many, which are too simple, offered. I think of the agrarian mythology, "a simple peaceful farming people" as George Washington liked to call us. Or I think of the suburban theology: two marigolds and a zinnia. Simple. Easy Maintenance. Look exactly like our neighbors. Or I think of nearly any fundamentalism that promises simplicity in exchange for interpreting your own reality.

Good garden theology is based in garden reality. Garden reality is tension, not harmony. Moses coveted grapes. Jesus went to the garden to weep. The Garden of Eden is our origin. People go to the garden alone while the dew is still on the meadows. There they pray and meditate; they walk and talk with God.

I think of Vita Sackville-West and May Sarton and Katharine White as my gardening theologians. Reading any of them is almost as good as a visit to a holy place. They manage the tension of the garden by showing us what is there that is holy and what is missing in the holy. Each of these women advises the gypsy in us. What is the gypsy? She is the restless part in us, the part that moves.

Gypsies tell us what they have learned by going the road themselves. They show us how full the garden is as spiritual source—and then they point to its frustrations. By doing both, they adhere us to our gardens and point us ever beyond them.

Gardening is a full enough experience to show us our own limitations. It is a light thrown on what is both full and partial in us. Gardening announces what we can and what we can't do. I can't grow sweet peas. Yet. I can't miss on greens. So far.

While each of my three gardening friends found enormous satisfaction in the garden, each also found disturbance. They mistrusted their love of the garden, knew that it was *just* a refuge from the more important and difficult world. As gypsies, they were suspicious of contentment.

The theology of the gypsy is here: part is whole. Limitation is normal. Suspicion is an aspect of trust. But never be satisfied with just part; go for the whole. Never get limited by suspicion; trust even suspicion. Keep moving toward something you know

you're not going to achieve. Gardening is a great laboratory for that kind of spiritual process; it substi-
tutes something temporal and small and specific for
something eternal and large and grand.

Many women use the garden theologically in these
ways. We find enjoyment there. We try to improve on
it but fortunately aren't able to. A similar partial journey through imperfection was the journey of these
three famous women as well. They longed for refuge
and then mistrusted it. They too remembered their
failures in the garden long after they had forgotten
their successes. They glimpsed eternity from a patch
of tulips.

Many women use Vita Sackville-West, Katharine
Anne White, and May Sarton as their spiritual mentors in the garden. We try to get spiritual and gardening guidance from them. A mentor is a supervisor
who risks becoming a friend; each of these women
does that, albeit in an almost icy way.

Mention the name of May Sarton, and many women
will say that she fully revealed the prize of solitude in
the garden. Mention the name of Katharine White,
and many women will say she taught them the art of
thinking about the garden. If Katharine was all mind
over matter, then our third mentor, Vita Sackville-
West was all matter over mind. Mention the name of
Vita, and many will say that she supervised their sexuality while making it look, for all practical purposes,
as though she were talking about gardening.

Gardens resurrect the spirit, the mind, and the body. That is their complete spirituality. Each of these women supervises one of these connections; Sarton, spirit, White, mind, Sackville-West, body. Not that Sarton doesn't understand sex, or Vita spirit, or Katharine a bit of all three, but rather that each has a particular window on the ways that dirt resurrects. Each has a spiritual specialty.

May Sarton can actually drive a person quite crazy with her urgency about solitude. On the one hand, she seems to have more friends and guests than anyone else. On the other, she seems quite unhappy to have them. She frets. If it rains the day after M. comes, then how will she get the tulips in? If she didn't have such successful books, then she would not have so little time in the garden. The garden brings her peace; the friends hassle. So why does she spend so much time with the friends and so little time in the garden? If there is an answer, Sarton will find it. God knows she is on its trail with all the energy she has. Like any gypsy, she keeps moving toward the answer without genuinely expecting to find it.

Likewise Katharine White was an overly productive person. She managed the *New Yorker* with its various writers, two children, a famous husband, and a sparkling literary life. Then as she and the *New Yorker* aged together, and it needed her less as years went by, she began to garden. Her husband describes her mingling manuscripts with seed and bulb, editing one

Angus Pettingill of White Flower Farms with the same dark pencil that she used on Thurber. She put on a suit in the morning and came out of the garden looking as officious as when she entered. Whether pruning or penciling, her hands remained busy. Her greatest gardening pleasure was the arrangement of the flowers for lunch. Once an editor, always an editor.

Katharine lusted after the product of the garden, its beauty, the filling up of space with colorful peace. May Sarton and Katharine White both give endless descriptions of windowsills cradling blossoms, of pages unwritten unless eyes are graced with flowers.

Why do I feel that entering either home would evoke the same sensibility? Calmed, coiled beauty, enduring no fools, welcoming while critiquing all comers? Are you, the guest would be subtly asked, a taker or a giver, good enough to enjoy these flowers or this mind?

Not one of these women was modest. Their gardens weren't modest, and they weren't modest. Each had a realistic assessment of her value. They were right not to nice their time away with the hoi polloi. That this absence of modesty indulged some of the worst freedoms of the rich is another matter. Class contains privileges, and some use the privilege class brings to expand leisure time. These three rich women used their privilege to grow flowers and, through flowers, to risk the constant resurrection of solitude, thought, and sexuality. The gypsy spirit knows that there are plenty of people being nice and too few risking practical resurrection.

Of course their freedom is an embarrassment to that other kind of woman writer, the one without domestic help or secretary. Katharine's complaint in one of her letters to May tells all: "Household and secretarial help, i.e., the lack of it, is my greatest enemy."

The theological linchpin for each woman is that she thought she deserved happiness, leisure, wealth, and fun. I am actually warmed by this expectation. It brings out the better gypsy, the better rover. We so rarely hear women of this stature whine. They complain instead. Poor and middle-class women would do well to imitate right here: to be more content with our high expectations for life rather than guilty about them. Such an attitude might not make us better gardeners, but it would make us better gypsies. And gypsies find God in the least likely places. God is not so much in the better places or the better expectations—or even in my awkwardly given advice in this paragraph. God is more likely to be found in the places we can't quite see. Yet God is in the gypsy stretch, urging us to take a step out into something we can't quite discern so that, from there, we can begin to see.

As I think about moving my garden north, I experience the most fear right here in the stretch. Can I really expect as good a garden in my next spot? Or as good a life? Or is one of the punishments of restlessness decreasing pleasure? That backhanded way in which fear tells you that you'd better stay put, because "a bird in the hand is worth two in the bush."

This kind of fear would not have stopped Katharine White. She would think her way through it. Nor would it have stopped Vita. She simply didn't understand boundaries well enough to respect them. May would have the fear, admit to having the fear, and then conquer it.

I am most fond of sexy Vita. She was neither more modest nor less rich than the other two. Still I imagine a warmer welcome to the stranger from her equally vivid windowsills. Vita was always in love. If not with Virginia Woolf, then with her husband or another of her male or female lovers. She had that kind of bilingual lust. Fortunately, for the snooty morality of England, she had a garden, too. The garden skimmed off some of the cream. You have the feeling, because of Vita, that gardening is most accessible through the body, not the mind or spirit.

In her garden the colors were bright, the privacy carefully planned, the refuge a top priority. When Vita fell out of love, it was to the three shades of cosmos that she went for comfort. Would she have understood as much of the peace of a garden without the lovers? No, it was the risky love she brought to the garden that animated it. Would any of the more prudent and prudish women understand her risky love? May, yes, because May is a lesbian who has to understand sexuality; Katharine probably not. Never forget that when May's vivid mind went to look for a metaphor to describe who Katharine was to her other women writers of the period, she chose the metaphor of Mother Superior. Katharine was our Mother Superior, she said. Less sexy you can't get.

Vita had more of the gypsy in her, and she saw probably more pictures of God through her body than mind or soul could capture. At Sissinghurst, Vita Sackville-West's castle home, her unconventional gardening ideas came into their own. First she practiced a kind of ruthlessness in her gardens. Never keep things that don't work. Don't give them another year or another chance. Hers was an unplanned garden, a spontaneous garden, one in which wild experimentation was always taking place. Her gardening columns for the *London Observer* endured from 1947 to 1961, showing that she had enough new ideas to carry on.

As a result of these several immodesties, we are all well mentored. We have some good, if not kind, friends. We have a few pictures of what the Resurrection looks like to a few good dreamers. To be shown the point of view of the mind opens the garden to evaluation, to reflection, to hard analysis of what best use to put to dirt, of what to let go and what to keep. These gardens make decisions about the last days and what belongs in them.

One of the ways in which each of these women is a gypsy is her discontent, her roving spirit, the way she was never quite satisfied right where she was.

Another is each one's specialization. If it is true, as I think, that Vita was more body than soul or mind, Katharine more mind than body or soul, and May more soul than body or mind, then the missing part is what is longed for in the garden. The discontent is directly related to the shadow rather than the ful-filled part.

Katharine frets over what to plant and when to plant. Vita frets over missing color. May frets over missing emotion, over what she calls in her book, *After the Stroke* (1988), time to watch the sun slide across her porch. The garden satisfies the part in each that it can satisfy and dissatisfies the part in each which is underdeveloped. Gypsy theology under-stands that we are all like this, only parts, only spokes, only able to see what we can see of God and garden and not really very much more.

Many people, and not just gypsies, are specialized to the point of eternal longing for what we don't have. Not quite happy right where we are. We can learn a little about the parts we don't have and even learn to use them, but we have to keep moving *north* or *south* to exercise them.

To be shown the point of view of the spirit is to for-give every garden's product for not being all that it might have been, to make a priority of the process, the gift of all that time alone, whether or not it panned out. The spirit sees in a fuzzy way. Through the fuzz, it sees beauty.

The mind clarifies. It sees very clear lines, demarcated plants, whole systems. The mind really does want to know what the soil test said. What type of nematode did what. It keeps records for succession planting.

To experience the body as it experiences the garden, not just as work but also as lust, is to connect to the earth, to adore it, to understand why recreation and procreation are so firmly partnered in sexual activity. This is why Christians say that we believe in the resurrection of the body, right before we mention life everlasting. To know the garden through the body is to touch it, caress it, not be able to pass by the peonies without giving them a wave.

Nevertheless, enter the gypsy's permanent dissatisfaction: wouldn't it be fun to combine the trinity into a unity, to have that richly erotic experience of the body, mind, and soul all being invited out to play in the same afternoon? Possible only in sex? Only in writing? Only in gardening? Only in heaven? Only in wishful conversation as mentors become friends? The answer is a yes to all the possibilities as long as you don't expect to see every one, every season. And as long as some afternoons, all you see is shadow.

Katharine is summed up by her husband E. B. White as every fall planting bulbs and "calmly plotting the Resurrection" (1979). Exactly! As women gardeners see it, the resurrection of the body and the spirit and the mind all develop from the holy dirt wholly experienced. Or they don't. They finally either do or don't. The gypsy knows what it means when perfection doesn't quite happen. She may even enjoy the not quite happening parts. It is from within the knowledge that it is not quite perfect that we go into the gypsy theological stretch. From that level of reality—which does take a mind, body, and soul to recognize that something is missing—we begin to see. That seeing is as much God as records well kept, sex well consummated, or light on a front porch well viewed. God may be all three. Gypsies can only be one at a time.

Gypsy theology is most astute in understanding matters of idolatry. Human is part, not whole. God is whole, not part. Gypsy gardeners aren't humbled by that. We are driven instead back to the garden.

22

SUMMER GARDENS
ON THE ISLES OF SHOALS

THE RITUALS OF RETREATS

I BOTH LOVE and hate to travel in the summer. So sums up the gypsy theory of life. Can't stay, can't go. To leave one's own garden in its hyperactive time is painful. The only balm is the ability to see another's garden. I go to Star Island and Appledore now regularly. They are islands of "Shoals" seven miles out to sea from Portsmouth, New Hampshire. There I imagine that Celia Thaxter's famous garden is mine. The fantasy comforts me till I get home.

This summer borrowing all began when I was called to be chaplain for a week at Star Island. I couldn't have picked a worse sermon topic for my six-day series at Family Camp if I had tried. "Hope in Hard Times" it was called. The first day I stood at the pulpit in the Gosport Chapel and stared out at the rock's intimacy with the ocean, all around. I remember thinking, "What hard times? Are there hard times somewhere? Is that possible?"

By boat, Star is a thirty dollar and one hour trip. The waves the Steamship Company calls moderate, most travelers experience as choppy. A good swell develops right out of the harbor, and that is the last time most people experience a hard time for their stay.

I was joining a United Church of Christ Family Camp. Others go for science camps, nature camps, or no-theme camps, and they usually stay for one week each. The cost of the camp is now about $500 per week and includes all meals, lodging, and program. Children come for half that and have organized activities most of the day.

I had come as volunteer staff and was much too selfish about the rest of my time on the island to redo my "Hope in Hard Times" series. Daily I asked for the worshippers' forgiveness. Forgive me for allowing the mainland to intrude so fiercely on the island. We are here, I argued, to "retrue" ourselves—as one of the painters who came here long ago said. Retrueing must mean at least making the connections to the beauty here and the hard times on the mainland. The argument either worked or it didn't. I rather forgot about my performance and cared about mica and majesty instead. Mica is the rock that the island is made of; the children are given hammers and they go off to chip away at it. The adults are given the majesty of the surrounding sea; we chip away at that as well.

The United Church of Christ and the Unitarian Universalists own Star Island and use it for "religious and educational purposes." College students, called Pelicans, retrieve your bags right at the boat, and you walk to the grand old hotel up the hill, bowing as you greet her and she invites you to take one of the rocking chairs on the porch. I chipped away at the majesty from one of those chairs most of the week.

Fifty-four feet above the high water mark, the hotel is white clapboard and makes you want to put on a long dress for dinner. The island, first mapped by Captain John Smith in 1614, is only forty-two acres but seems as large as all outdoors. Horizons of the Atlantic on one side and a bright New Hampshire and Massachusetts coastline on the other turn the trick of creating space out of succinctness.

At our Mini Chautauqua, one of over a dozen held each summer, week by week, the theme was Family Values. I came almost to believe in them again in the silent procession up the rocky path to the meeting-house in the dark for the candlelight service that ends the day. The wrought-iron hooks waited all day for the processional of light; once the lanterns were hung, and the music begun, electrified thoughts from the mainland met their nemesis.

So fond did I become of my forgetfulness from shore that I even forgot self-improvement. There were many events in which I did not even participate. The daily polar bear swims that did not rise above sixty-five degrees were replaced by a cup of tea. I preferred the rather loud bell in the buoy to the sound of my teeth chattering. I wanted to focus all my attention on creation, not recreation. The bridge games and the tennis tournaments—on a truly awful court—part of Star's non-resort appeal, or the wildflower walks, and the open sings sounded too much like appointments, starting as they did, at specified times. I coveted the island clocklessness too much to do what I otherwise might have enjoyed.

I took full advantage of the excellent daily child-care provided by two long-term staff people who, in their shore life, educate Boston's children. My three cherubs spent their days mica mining on the rocks, exploring pirate caves, and hearing scary stories of times of yore. (It seems, in fact, that one Betty Moody, a first white settler, hid in a cave from genuine pirates and smothered her newborn to death while protecting her.) They reported these tales to me at the three excellent meals per day we shared—and then took off. Forgive me also if I describe these brief visits, replete with excited narrative, as my ideal of childcare.

Star is one of nine islands in a group known as the Isles of Shoals. "Shoals" is an old English word for school of fish. Historian Fred McGill, a retired English professor who first visited Star in 1922 and has been back yearly ever since for the entire season, tells of what Star does to him. "It roots me. Funny isn't it, how all this tide could make you feel stable?"

Pelicans, the college-age staffers, don't just bear the bags up the hill. They put on a superb talent show—hired as they are by needing to bring one talent or skill as well as a need for a summer job—and only choose one day a week to do cross-dressing in the dining room. Their sense of humor needs to be large: the guests are dependent on them to lug morning pitchers of wash water for their rooms. They must really appreciate faucets when they return to school.

If there is a difficulty at Star, it is water. Two showers a week are all the guests are permitted. In the morning, the Pelicans bring hot cistern water to the rooms in plastic buckets. So much of what is old-fashioned is pleasant; this feature is not, but is forgotten very soon, especially after everyone else's hair in the dining room starts looking a lot like yours.

The poison ivy is a seriously unmajestic aspect of the creation as are the seagulls. Much of the island is a biological tangle of briar and wild cherry, witch grass, and sumac, evidence of how much people have left it alone and God has allowed nature to carry on.

To keep the seagull population down, phony eggs have been placed around the island. These eggs trick the gulls into thinking they are having babies. More than just the Audubon Society cares what happens to birds on the island. There are times when the population of seagulls has seriously interfered with the mica mining of the children and the morning walks of the adults. Not wanting to upset the balance of nature in the place, nor to let the seagulls prohibit human use of the island, many methods of population control have been used on the island. The phony egg method has worked, so far.

Star is the wilder of the islands in the Isles of Shoals. For horticulture you have to boat from Star to Appledore, a short trip across the harbor. There the famous Celia Thaxter garden exists. She is surely the most famous of the Shoals residents. Thaxter was a gifted writer, passionate romantic, and uncommon gardener. When it came time to restore her garden, former Islanders came from throughout New England, returning sprigs and seeds, bulbs and ideas, all of which their parents and grandmothers had borrowed from Appledore. The garden is now completely its old self. Sort of.

The hops vine on both Star and Appledore, as well as the tawny day lily, are Thaxter signatures. Despite more than seventy years of neglect, John Kingsbury, founding director of the Shoals Marine Laboratory on Appledore, was able to reconstruct the small garden completely in the last few decades. He even used Celia's old method of planting slips in eggshells and then burying them in the ground. There are people all over New England who have day-tripped to Appledore to leave old-fashioned plants or to pick them up. In their purses they carry the eggshells.

Thaxter grew up on the Isles of Shoals, first on White Island, where as a lonely child, she grew marigolds, later on Appledore, where her family opened a resort hotel. At sixteen she wed her tutor, Levi Thaxter, a dreamer eleven years her senior. The marriage was difficult from the start and filled with lengthy separations. Celia filled her days with writing and gardening.

In her newly popular book, *An Island Garden*, she says, "Mine is just a little old-fashioned garden where the flowers come together to praise the Lord" (1988). When she thought of praise, color, not layout, was her primary concern. The contrast of her bright colors with the island's varying bleached shades is truly spectacular.

Attracted in the last century to her place by her unassuming charm, such luminaries as Impressionist Childe Hassam, poet James Russell Lowell, and authors William Dean Howells, and Harriet Beecher Stowe made annual pilgrimages. When she died in 1894, her family maintained the garden for a few years but eventually left the island. In 1914 a fire destroyed her hotel complex and her cottage, then the garden disappeared. Now the fifty by fifteen foot garden looks as it did in the beginning. Searching antique catalogs for the plant names and acquiring the roots from specialized nurseries, the Marine Laboratory was able to put things back together. The garden is open to the public only by permission from June to September by calling the Marine Lab at the Isle of Shoals.

Whenever, as a gypsy, you need to borrow another's garden for a while, here on Appledore there is one waiting for you. It is a wild place, mostly because of the hovering of the gulls. But Celia packed it with color. She tried to stabilize the wild island and did so for a few brief years at the hotel. But the wild won. The hotel burned down in an amazing blaze in the twenties, and no one dared rebuild it. The garden's disrepair has now been changed, but people now must see it surrounded by *nature* as opposed to *civilization*, whatever that distinction means.

The spiritual experience of Star is equally wild, equally unusual. Nathaniel Hawthorne knew it as that "stern and awful place" (Thaxter, 1988). More than one family vacation has been interrupted by the sternness of the place. At Family Camp this year, on his birthday, seven-year-old Joshua told some of the story of his birth. His mother delivered him seven years ago on the last day of Family Camp, after a quick Coast Guard ride home. Jordan, another camper was equally lucky but not immediately. When he got hit in the head with a baseball bat, on a morning when the whole camp was fogged in, the Coast Guard was finally able to get him to a mainland hospital that afternoon. He survives now with medication for his seizures. People call that the longest day on Star Island. Classes and chapel were canceled while people waited for the Coast Guard boat, or the fog to lift.

There are hard times, even on Star. Very few gardens grow simply. Most are as complex as growth or birth itself. Just like the education for religion that is supposed to be going on. And the chaplains who come in from time to time, to address the wrong subject, in their spare time.

Even, and especially, the gypsy gardener has to have hope. Hope for the delicate is hard to sustain when we don't see the long-term rewards for our efforts. Seeing Celia Thaxter's garden live and die and be reborn gave me hope for the delicate.

That hope had been particularly beaten down by own experience I had in my Long Island, New York, garden. There in the south garden, all the weeds went to military school and the flowers all went to finishing school. Peonies, sweet peas, and poppies are not strong enough to stand up to that green thing with the blue flowers only in the morning. It had taken over every year and smashed the lighter flowers to smithereens.

A smart gardener would have called the south garden the "green-thing-with-the-blue-flowers-only-in-the-morning garden" and left it at that. I ordered sweet pea seed.

My husband thinks it is my excessive openness to weeds, my lack of early pulling that causes this war between fragility and toughness to happen in more than just the south garden. Like the mentally ill man who painted our house, sort of, that summer. He made the toughness of gardening seem mild.

I think it's a decision not to let the weeds go into the harsh world alone and uncomforted. It is also a choice to show all the sides of God and garden. It is actually a hope for the delicate.

One choice, under these circumstances, is to plant only nasturtiums. They wave the same in the breeze as sweet peas and have an equal lightness. They might have more of a chance against the green thing, and they don't require the soil to be fussed with so before planting. If anything, they like a poverty-stricken soil, insufficient moisture, and weird trace elements. Sweet peas are just the opposite. Only a well-laden, richly fed table for them. If their wine glass is empty, even between courses, they die.

But the nasturtiums are too easy. When they survive, there is comfort in it. Like a child born for school and raised in a home where books are everywhere, their victories come too easily. As a gardener, I prefer the tougher cases—if for no other reason than to magnify the miracle of growing, to see it on its true terms. Like the man who sort of painted the house, the delicate species enjoy a larger success. You have to measure their progress from the point at which they started, not from the point at which the average person or plant starts.

My patron saint in these matters is Celia Thaxter. She gardened in one of the most hostile environments imaginable. If Celia can grow poppies and sweet peas on what Hawthorne called the island's "bare-blown rock" (Thaxter 1988), then I can grow them in the south garden.

There is no point in wearing a hat on Appledore. It will blow off. Sundresses are equally frivolous. A sturdy sweatshirt is what you'll need. And yet, Celia, eight miles out, grew poppies. Shirley poppies to be exact. She started all her seedlings in eggshells. More fragile you cannot get. When she heard that toads were good at prohibiting certain pests, she ordered a breed from France! This purchase, before the days of UPS, which might itself have trouble getting the toads to Appledore, is an act of courage on behalf of the garden. Just the logistics of it all bother me.

But they did not bother Celia. Her favorite plant was the sweet pea. Blue, rose, pink, and white, The idea of those sweet peas battling the ocean wind is enough to inspire any gardener. Hollyhocks you can understand, although even these, another Thaxter signature, don't like to be blown about once they get tall.

The delicate need courage more than the strong. The strong have their strength. The delicate have miracles behind them. When James Russell Lowell commented that here, on Appledore, "you are so near to the great heart of God that you can almost hear it beat" (Thaxter, 1988), I wonder what he meant. Was he referring to the great and almighty wind, the all-mighty, all-powerful, all-knowing, the one we call the everything God—and some of us call the totalitarian—or might he have been referring to the strength in the tides? Or the severity of the rock? Or, might he have been referring to delicate beauty, colored petals that survive the storms, which lift up after being beaten down? Might he have seen clear through to the heart of God, that place where the weak, miraculously, are protected?

He could also be talking about the multiple personalities of the divine. Hollyhocks that bend with the wind and those that topple, Shirley poppies and that green thing that only blooms in the morning. It's hard to say. We can never really know which God another sees. Celia thought you could get toads to Appledore and did; my painter thought he couldn't paint and didn't.

Of course Celia kept her flowers short. To do otherwise was to tempt both wind and fate beyond the risky limit she already challenged. She also kept her garden small, fifty feet by ten feet, a riot of delicate color but concise, to the point, not roaming beyond the safety of a hill above and a hill below. The tall-green-thing-with-the-blue-flowers-only-in-the-morning would not make it here. It would be blown over by the first Nor'easter. Not to mention that its proportion of green and growth to blue and needly was too small. You have to bloom vigorously to stay in the delicate garden.

If there is to be hope for the delicate, you probably also need a particular kind of gardener. Almost Godlike, the type that is off rounding up lost sheep. Listen to Celia's self-description: "I garden to love up. To nourish. To cherish things into health and vigor" (1988). This from a woman who spent sleepless nights over the matter of slugs. It is dangerous to be delicate. You need protection. You need a gardener who doesn't mind the softer verbs of "nourish" and "cherish," those words that have the same strong sound of a heartbeat, the same sound of sweet peas whispering in the soft breeze. The delicate have no hope if all the gardener can do is hoe and dig, rake and stake. But the delicate have hope, even in my south garden, if they intend to whisper the word "miracle" and to do that to the breeze. One summer I returned to Star to teach a gardening course. Everything we planted failed to survive the winter. It was embarrassing.

All these lessons I would not have known had I not found the pain of being away from my own garden in the summer. The gypsy gets things that those who stay at home can never imagine. She retreats as a homing device.

23

GARDENING AT NIGHT

The Ritual of the Dark

THE LATEST THING in gardening is lighting the night. There is actually a night light store near me, and every gardening catalogue I receive has a more elegant display of lampposts than the last. I have been gardening in the dark for so many years now that I find this trend catching up to me more than I to it.

When you know that you are a gypsy, and not just one in the garden, you know that gardening is something you can do anywhere, anytime. I have been known to weed the Marriot parking lot. I have also gone in search of the green at convention centers. I no longer evaluate their landscaping services, but I do make sure I find out what bow they have made to what they call nature amidst their concrete. I travel a lot and often find myself far from my own garden.

When I am at home, I garden at night because I work all day and because I have an absurd discipline requiring me to touch soil daily. I count a day lost in which I don't touch the garden.

By that I mean, on a bad day, touching it and pulling two weeds; on a good day, giving an hour to some worthy plot. This discipline has kept me alive to the soil and allowed what would otherwise be an unmanageable garden to be unmanageable in a more interesting way. The discipline keeps garden in the category of prayer: it is my rug. If I can't get there five times a day, I can bow to it at least once.

Often in the darker seasons of fall and winter, I find myself moving rabbit manure at twilight, or pulling up stakes at midnight, or hoeing while the moon comes up. I make no claim for fertility added or earned by night gardening, but I know that an Aztec or Mayan would. They would garden at night for the advantages; I do it for the conveniences.

In the 1300s the belief was widely circulated that humans are wiser when the moon is waxing, and therefore any work needing thought, such as planning a layout, should be done at that time. Greek and Roman gardeners believed that the moon affected plants because the sap would wax and wane with the changing phases. Now we know that tides and moons are connected, then they only just assumed it. More than one person plants by horticultural horoscope, which strikes me as just another way of stating personal convenience.

Surely more majesty was deposited during Creation than we could ever, in our scientific mode, imagine. There was more order, more intention, more interplay in the genetic disposition of things than even prayer and praise can comprehend. When I plant at night, after a long day of other kinds of work, I am connecting my life to these original mysteries. I am insisting that soil touch me, that night and day differentiate me, that the daring of creation be something I remember. I am a pilgrim back to that second day, when darkness took the name of night and light the name of day.

My days are otherwise a conspiracy to make me forget that I am created, ordered, intended, even genetically mysterious. In the day, gardening reminds me of the enormity of creation. But at night, with stars as my guide, I am creation's participant-observer, kin to the divine, illuminated, re-created.

Certain constellations have compelled the human mind since the beginning of time. We think of Orion or Ursa Major. We say that science and mathematics had their origin in the questions posed by the night. No doubt religion has its own settling of accounts with the questions of the night. By day I work on these as a recession-beleaguered pastor. At night, in my garden, I co-create when I'm not gazing at the stars. Or being held spellbound by the moonlight. Or imagining the time when, once again, gardening will be as natural as my day job.

24

THE MATTER OF WEEDS

THE RITUAL OF IMPROVEMENT

THERE ARE ALWAYS weeds. They are everywhere. Pulling a couple gives that sense of satisfaction that the gardener lives for, and also has a sneaky way of keeping that activity known as *weeding* a part-timer in your garden. I would so much rather move the strawberries, or dead-head the petunias as a day's gardening activity, than go *weeding*. Weeding brings us up to the place we should have been; other garden activities take us somewhere. If I have to weed, I like to do it at night. We can't stay long in the night garden. We will get involved in the stars soon enough and find our way back into our covers. Going utilitarian before the stars grab us is always a good idea.

Weeding gives us more than a quick utility and a long star gaze. It provides more than connection to the ancients who respected both light and dark equally. Weeding as gardening has a kind of poetry. We both see the big weeds—and pull them—and don't see the little ones. "Poets are rich in points of view if they are rich in anything." So says Robert Francis in his poem dedicated to the Juniper tree. Weeding increases our points of view. It replenishes our stock of garden memories for the next day.

Weeding is not a falsified viewpoint. It is not like make-up that a sour face puts on to look better. Weeding gets some forms of beauty out of the way of the beauty you intended in the garden. Some weeds are more beautiful than some flowers. Discerning which is which can be very important.

There is an enormous field on the corner of Northville Turnpike and Route 58 in Riverhead, New York. It is probably the most accessible open space within walking distance of my old house. Something new is happening there every season. The field can brim with St. Johnswort, daisies, dandelions, crab-grass, timothy, clover, pigweed, lamb's quarters, but-tercup, mullein, Queen Anne's lace, plantain, and yarrow. Or it can sprout grasses too numerous to name. But each does have a name. Not one of these species was here before the Puritans landed. And now they threaten to take us over.

According to Sara B. Stein's *My Weeds* (1988), wild oats growing in a field of alternating furrows of spring and winter barley will mimic the habits of either crop, depending on the row. She also tells of a rice mimic that became so troublesome that researchers planted a purple variety of rice to expose the weeds once and for all. Within a few years, the weed-rice had turned purple too. At night we can't see all these costumes. But we see others. And knowing what these plants are really up to amazes us even more as they turn in the lights of the night.

Not to respect weeds is to refuse a message from the divine, the message that nature is unbelievably smart and resilient, that plants mean to survive. That message may not relieve all of our burdens, but surely when it comes to the big one about our own survivability, we should take a little comfort in the million miracles of the weeds.

The botanical fact about weeds is that they grow in response to human disturbance. The more humans disturb the environment, the more the weeds adapt and grow. Another botanist, Jack Harlan, in *Crops and Man* says, "If we confine the concept of weeds to species adapted to human disturbance, then man is by definition the first and primary weed under whose influence all the other weeds have evolved" (1992).

Ralph Waldo Emerson saw the same thing. He said that a weed is simply a plant whose virtues we haven't yet discovered. Other people have been less kind about the weed. Paul Dickson says that when weeding, the best way to make sure what you are pulling is a weed and not a valuable plant is to pull on it. If it comes out of the ground easily, it is a valuable plant. Learning to respect what we don't want, didn't plant, can't get rid of—this is the ritual of the activist gardener, the one who keeps shaping what can't really be shaped.

25

SEED CATALOGUES

THE RITUAL OF HOPE

THE CLYDE ROBIN Seed Company sent me its 1990 wildflower catalogue from Castro Valley, California. The catalogue arrived on one of those late winter days that needed outside intervention. I remember both the rain and the fog and their implication that gray was in charge. The cover of the catalogue gave my resistance movement the little push it needed. I am a member of an international resistance movement against the grays. We need all the help we can get. When reality dampens, fantasy is required.

There on the cover was a marvelous specimen of a California woman, kneeling, knee-deep in yellow poppies and blue flax. She had the look of health all over her face: the white hair that peeped out from under her hat exuded vitamins, her tailored outfit announced that she was in this for fun. (Farm workers are different from gardeners in at least this way: they don't get dressed up to pick.) Behind the sloping field of yellow, in conversation with blue, was a trellis that led, Zenlike, down another slope to the cottage. Implied in this photo was the idea that this grand lady lived in this humble cottage. At her breakfast table were melon and whole grains; in an ancient pitcher made for poppies and flax, flowers graced her meal. She didn't stop to pray, having prayed without ceasing since the day began, so caught was her eye in beauty each minute. On that winter day when gray was king at my cottage and this colorful catalogue spilled out of my mail, I nearly ordered a pound of poppy seeds. And they don't even grow in my New York climate!

Another day, more modest in its threat to our movement, Jackson and Perkins "Home Gardening Excellence Since 1872" showed up in the mail. Jackson and Perkins have made their name recently by selling a cheap variety of hardy fence roses, the color of which is certainly not gray but has that repeatable, interchangeable quality that is threatening to become one position above gray. Since everyone in nearly every community has bought these fast-growing pink roses, the world is beginning to format to a Jackson and Perkins color code. We need to resist these conformities when and as we can. First it was marigolds and now this!

Jackson and Perkins in this new edition was moving on, beyond the roses. Their cover was cottage garden. The house behind the cottage had its door seductively open to show an easel and a few paints. People in these houses don't do dishes or have dustballs under their couches. They spend their days painting and gardening. If we buy items from these catalogues, perhaps we may enjoy the same leisure.

J and P wants to sell me a hammock from that now-famous Pauley's Island, wicker, infantile garden sculptures, planters that are much more respectable and expensive than the recyclables I now use, botanical prints, English picnic baskets, and some delightful astilbes. Clearly they are trying to move up a notch in social class. The astilbes come in both a pink and a white feathery style that demonstrate the genuine concern J and P has for color and its variations. I not only should, but did, order them, and they were worth the $6.95 per. They have a respect for the variety of pinks that our movement need not fear paying for.

Now that we have established the importance of fantasy and the importance of color to our resistance movement against the bland, the gray, and the conforming, we are ready for Gardener's Supply which offers innovative gardening solutions. These people imply by their slogan that there are problems in gardening, and there are. We need the pragmatist to round out our little sermon. Gardener's Supply sells a variety of hoses, planters, fertilizers, kneelers, edgers, teepees, and sakes, composters—even one described as the Cadillac of composters, tools to stir up composters, shredders, etc. These tools give our movement the kind of infrastructure it needs if it is to be taken seriously. By calling or writing them in Burlington, Vermont, you can outfit yourself for the long haul of making fantasy and color survive. That they provide free environmental gardening bulletins shows that they not only have products that sustain us, but they are also aware of sustainability as a public value. Of course, you can always stir your homemade compost pile with a stick and sustain yourself that way, too.

Now it is summer, and I'm glad for the astilbes that I ordered instead of all those poppies. I really like my compost stirrer. I enjoyed these items when I ordered them, and I am enjoying them now. Spring is clearly the foreplay to summer's sex. Then we hoped, now we realize hope.

By fall we will be remembering these realized hopes and stocking our arsenal against the inevitable return of the gray. Photographs are a good weapon. That's one of the things the seed catalogues return to tell us in the spring. They snap flax and poppies and California women at their peak. They wait till the dishes are done and the easel properly set up to click their cameras on the finest day August provides. They put on their boots on days when there is no mud and line them up on fancy doormats, thereby selling us tools to sustain our movement.

I have two photos on my desk. They are not orgasmic memories but rather arrows in the quiver of my resistance. One is just a bunch of zinnias, arranged on the porch of a beach house a friend loaned me one year. The zinnias are set between the two rocking chairs on which we sat to view the bay. I can look over when I am writing and rock a little despite the fact that the zinnias only lasted three good days.

The other photo is of my two sons in shirtless overalls, running down a Vermont hill late in August and early in their life. They are holding hands. Yes, these are the same two boys who ouch each other every day but not always in affectionate ways. They are running toward the garden with the green beans we ate that night for supper. Over the hill a bit are the Green Mountains, shouting resistance, covered with wildflowers sufficient for a lifetime of color and fantasy. The picture doesn't show all this. It just reminds me that it is there, and that at least one summer I saw it. Now these photos sustain me against the return of the gray.

Without the seed catalogues, far too many pictures would be lost. The grays would win the battle against hope. Because of the pictures, hope wins.

26

THE RETURN OF
THE PUSH MOWER

THE RITUAL OF ESCHATOLOGICAL THINKING

THE WOMAN WITH the great hair in Miami became normal. Everybody started mowing their own lawns again and growing their own food. It is hard to say just how the anti-lawn, pro-garden movement got started. Or why it was that the push mower came back.

The devastation from global warming certainly got people's attention. And the third of the population disappearing made a difference. Living without cars just changed people.

The beginning, before the catastrophes, people say was on Father's Day late in the last century. Someone published a piece in the paper of record suggesting that the White House Lawn be abolished. The environmentalists had long been screaming about fertilizers and how they wash off the lawn into the wells and oceans, fouling up one balance after another. The fitness types gave up their power lawn mowers for aerobic purposes easily a decade earlier, and this loss of the capacity to maintain a bright green had already made the lawn smaller. One man, the father of the man who managed to suggest abolishing the White House lawn, actually mowed his initials in the weeds in front of his house because his neighbors complained so loudly about the mess he called his front yard.

When gas first went to five dollars a gallon, lawn mowing took on a new cachet. Only the rich could afford big lawns. Pachysandra companies took over chemical fertilizer companies, and most people made a rough adjustment to the new realities of crabgrass. But not without a vintage form of suburban anguish.

Some people still want a little lawn. They could give up the chemicals in favor of a less vivid green altogether. The gender politics of lawn mowing also played a part. Men were helping women with the dishes and diapers much more than women were helping men with the lawn. The Betty Friedan of the men's movement was never found but still, men's consciousness-raising groups flowered nationwide. Women were put on notice: men were not going to waste all their leisure time mowing even little lawns.

The decision to buy stock in push mowers was a crucial one for the men's movement. They watched women try to start power motors and knew that there would be no justice without a more appropriate technology. Women, oddly, agreed.

Most people credit Joe and Amy Ferguson with the real return of the push mower. Their pioneering family laid the groundwork for all the others; the story, now embellished, is this:

Amy had agreed with Joe about the justice of sharing lawn mowing. No matter how much fun her friends made of her for not being feminine enough, by God, she meant to mow the lawn. But every time she went outside to mow, she was frustrated by the power mower. She tried to start it, her younger son tried to start it, and her oldest son tried to start it. Like most of the men who had ever been in her life, these two offspring couldn't bear the sight of her being mechanical. Thus they made man-sounding noises and yanked on the lawn mower chain. Amy yanked on it with equal effort and no noises. Nothing happened. Joe came out and yanked on it with both boys gazing fondly at his muscles, listening eagerly for his noises. Still nothing happened. When he became hysterical and mumbled spark plugs over and over—realizing that there was no freedom if he had to still master the machine—Amy made her decision. She would get a lawn mower that she could push. She would not bother Joe anymore. He had learned detergents, she would learn mowing.

She went to three hardware stores in search of a push mower. Three times she was turned down. First by someone who, between chews, indicated that there wasn't much call for them anymore. The second guy actually laughed at her. The third guy looked at her ring finger and just shook his head. She had to endure disparagement of Joe. At the fourth store the man thought he had one left somewhere and, sure enough, he produced it, in a box, which she knew meant trouble.

The box meant that it wasn't standing up, and if it wasn't standing up, that meant she would have to bother poor old Joe with it. The whole point of this expedition was to keep him out of it. She didn't want to take a whole course in screwdrivers and bolts, so she told the salesman she'd take it if he'd find somebody to put it together. He said, "five dollars more." She said, "Sold!" He said, "Don't you want to see it first?" and she said, "Of course not." She didn't need to fondle it, just use it.

She did tell Joe that had she been more of a person, while those hardware store men were cautiously discussing the assembly with each other and doing a little bit of it at the same time, she would have gotten out her nail file, sat on an air-conditioner box and done her nails. Just for the effect. Each man had assured the other that he didn't know too much about these old machines *but* they got it together. Fifteen minutes later, Joe's wife was home and mowing. No muss, no fuss. No gas, no spark plugs. No husbands to program. Her glee was girlish and unbounded.

Both of her boys (but not her daughter) insisted on a turn behind the mower. She refused their request. Blowing hard, getting her heart rate way above its Wednesday morning aerobic level, she mowed the lawn. It was sheer bliss. Clack, clack, clatter, clatter. Except for having to move the curious kids vigorously out of the way every now and then, there were no obstacles. What she enjoyed most was the sound of the engine. There was no sound to the engine. None at all. Joe wasn't bothered either by the kids or the noise. He was peacefully watching the ball game, having finished folding the laundry. Amy couldn't have been more pleased.

Until their neighbor appeared. He came over and demanded to know what she was doing. Clearly he was concerned that Joe might be embarrassed by what his wife was doing right on the front lawn. The neighbor was so offended for Joe that he not only asked the question, he came over the next day and redid the area she had mowed with his riding power mower. Yes, he did. When Joe came home the next afternoon, sure enough, there he was riding over their mowed lawn. Joe was astonished. Imagine a guy like that being so hung up on his own masculinity that he couldn't let his wife enjoy a little power, a little exercise, a little relaxation.

It was the radical pioneering of Joe and Amy Ferguson, against all obstacles, in the early part of the twenty-first century, which led to the tradition of buying push mowers for fathers on Fathers Day. Or so say the anti-pachysandra people.

Now that people use their yards to grow food because they can't get it anywhere else, many wonder if the lawn will ever come back at all. Most keep the lawn mowers around just in case.

DONNA SCHAPER is Senior Minister of Judson
Memorial Church, Principal in "Bricks Without
Straw" Consulting Service for Social Change
Congregations and Not for Profits, mother of three
children, author of twenty-eight books, and happiest
when she is in the garden.